The Imperial Style of Inquiry in Twentieth-Century China

The Imperial Style of Inquiry in Twentieth-Century China

The Emergence of New Approaches

Donald J. Munro
The University of Michigan

CENTER FOR CHINESE STUDIES
THE UNIVERSITY OF MICHIGAN
ANN ARBOR

Open access edition funded by the National Endowment for the Humanities/ Andrew W. Mellon Foundation Humanities Open Book Program.

MICHIGAN MONOGRAPHS IN CHINESE STUDIES
ISSN 1081-9053
SERIES ESTABLISHED 1968
VOLUME 72

Published by
Center for Chinese Studies
The University of Michigan
Ann Arbor, Michigan 48109-1290

First Edition 1996

Printed and bound by CPI Group (UK) Ltd, Croydon, CR0 4YY

♾ The paper used in this publication meets the minimum requirements of the American National Standard for Information Sciences—Permanence of Paper for Publications and Documents in Libraries and Archives ANSI/NISO/Z39.48—1992.

Library of Congress Cataloging-in-Publication Data

Munro, Donald J.
The imperial style of inquiry in twentieth-century China :
the emergence of new approaches /
Donald J. Munro — 1st ed.
p. cm. —
(Michigan monographs in Chinese studies, ISSN 1081-9053 ; v. 72)
Includes bibliographical references and index
ISBN 0-89264-120-7 (alk. paper)
1. Inquiry (Theory of knowledge)
2. Social epistemology—China.
3. China—Civilization—20th century.
I. Title. II. Series.
Michigan monographs in Chinese studies ; no. 72
BD183.M86 1996
181′.11—dc20 96-256
CIP

ISBN 978-0-89264-120-8 (hardcover)
ISBN 978-0-472-03824-4 (paper)
ISBN 978-0-472-12782-5 (ebook)
ISBN 978-0-472-90178-4 (open access)

Derived from the author's
Distinguished Senior Faculty Lectures,
presented in 1994 on the occasion
of his receipt of the
Warner G. Rice Humanities Award,
College of Literature, Science, and the Arts,
The University of Michigan

For Betty, Cynnie, and Ellie.

Contents

Contents

Preface

This book examines the endurance in modern China of old philosophical ideas about knowledge and inquiry. These ideas are rooted in Neo-Confucian doctrines. They coexist along with other, different ideas about and approaches to the project and process of inquiry. The book also examines the impact of those ideas on problem solving. This includes the influence of philosophical ideas on proposing solutions to social or technical problems. Such solutions often have political policy implications. If the tone of the first three chapters is critical of old ideas as obstructions to inquiry, the last two are optimistic. They focus on signs of departure that I suggest will facilitate the solving of social problems.

Early in the book I describe Chinese totalism, a Confucian belief that there is an ordered structure integrating everything that exists; the same order runs through both the human and natural spheres. This belief justifies imperial authority by making the emperor responsible for the harmony of all the related parts. Totalism also supports a theory about the investigation of things that is highly authoritarian. It centers on copying antecedent models, whose ultimate legitimacy comes from the emperor. The models ensure that any particular situation under study will be understood in terms of the officially recognized, integrated totality.

This theory about the investigation of things also prizes clarifying the mind so it can intuit in itself the innate patterns that structure the world. Patterns in the human mind are believed to parallel in totality the actual patterns in nature, a belief that owes much to the Neo-Confucian Zhu Xi (1125-1200). These patterns provide information that is both descriptive and prescriptive, about how things predictably do and should behave. This is an aspect of what I call the fact-value fusion. I first discussed this phenomenon in historical context in chapter 2 ("The Nature of Mind") of my book, *The Concept of Man in Contemporary China* (Ann Arbor: University of Michigan Press, 1977). The idea of a fact-value fusion plays a significant role in the present book.

I call this Confucian theory about the investigation of things the "imperial style of inquiry," because it had the imperial imprimatur from 1313 until 1911, embodied in the authority of the philosophy of Zhu Xi and the *Four Books* of Confucianism for civil service examination purposes. It also assumes the emperor's role in maintaining the harmony of the whole. Sometimes I will refer to it as the "Confucian style of inquiry."

I will criticize those aspects of the belief in an integrated totality that lead investigators to seek in nature what are really only human traits and to expect to find in nature what are exclusively human values. I also criticize aspects of the reliance on antecedent models in inquiry.

I want to prevent two dangerous but possible misunderstandings about the positions I take in this study. The first is that I affirm both the possibility and desirability of separating in every way the realms of humans and of nature. In fact, I do not. Rather, I affirm the interdependency of the two: what happens to one usually affects the other, and humans can indeed act so as to improve the ecological health of living things. What I reject is the inference from interdependency that the so-called essential traits of humans and nature are the same. Doubtless some traits overlap, but humans are purposive, evaluating beings; we are conscious of hierarchy. I reject the attribution of hierarchy, purpose, and other value traits to nature and try to show that such attributions inhibit objective inquiry. My critique applies equally to China and to Europe.

The other potential misunderstanding is that I advocate the elimination of existing values from the process of inquiry in China and favor instead the substitution of liberal democratic American ones. In fact, I do not believe that it is desirable or possible to eliminate received values from the minds of those doing problem solving. What I favor is the incorporation of epistemic values consistent with the goals of science into the problem-solving process. I reject political or social values imposed by those with political power. Sometimes there is overlap in the terminology or content used to describe the epistemic values and the liberal democratic ones, but they are not identical. "Freedom" and "autonomy" are common to both. For example, the value of free and open communication and dissemination of information is consistent with scientific goals; so is individual autonomy in judging facts. In succeeding pages, I will try to make the case that developments in China fostering such autonomy are consistent with scientific inquiry. It is precisely on this matter of autonomy that critics will think I am most vulnerable, and so it requires special attention here.

A critic's potential misunderstanding will rest on the belief that I am advocating some value within Western individualistic ethics as a substitute for collectivist Confucian or Maoist values. This would mean that I am advocating individual autonomy as an intrinsic value, worth pursuing and prizing for its own sake. It might mean that I favor unconventional thinking or acting for its own sake. In fact, I advocate nothing of the kind. I am promoting individual autonomy as an instrumental value, worthwhile because it contributes to the *social* nature of inquiry. When a multitude of individuals feel free to put forth their own hypotheses about a problem, this generates a variety of hypotheses rather than just a few. Individual autonomy provides the motivation for individuals to formulate and study powerful hypotheses. It is the necessary condition for variability in the theories put forth. Variability does not exist if there is one model or one authority that dictates or sponsors a single official hypothesis. With variability, if people are working on the same problem, they can learn from each other's perspectives. People today speak of the cognitive division of labor. Investigators compete, following different angles, and usually achieve some advancement of knowledge. In his book, *The Advancement of Science,*[1] Philip Kitcher has a chapter entitled, "The Organization of Cognitive Labor." He says,

> The general problem of social epistemology, as I conceive it, is to identify the properties of epistemically well-designed social systems, that is, to specify the conditions under which a group of individuals, operating according to various rules for moderating their individual practices, succeed, through their interactions, in generating a progressive sequence of consensus practices.[2]

Elsewhere he remarks that "... scientists' social involvement with one another does not interfere with the employment of epistemically virtuous individual reasonings."[3]

In short, inquiry is social as well as individual, with many people competing and learning from each other. The end product is usually a collective one. This collective process of inquiry is most robust when there is variability in the theories that compete. That variability depends on individual autonomy in inquiry and reasoning. In this sense, we can treat such autonomy as an instrumental good, a means to good inquiry. It is not the same as regarding self-governance or unconventional thinking as good in itself, as some liberals might propose.

This is a position that opposes single models and single authorities, but does not oppose the authority of peers. Insofar as the individual's own particular needs may affect the hypotheses he initially proposes, there is a necessary place for peer evaluations and corrections.

I applaud the emergence of individual autonomy as a social value that coexists with, but does not replace, traditional collectivist social values. Recent systematic theoretical works on autonomy and less systematic popular expressions of it are the subject of chapter 5. I applaud these developments not because I favor substituting Western individualism for enduring Chinese values. To repeat, I do not think such a substitution is possible or desirable. I do so because I believe these developments are necessary historical precursors for individual autonomy to be accepted as a legitimate part of the social process of inquiry.

This book deals primarily with Chinese theories of inquiry as they relate to human problems. The people whose ideas concern me, be they in or out of politics, are writing as philosophers and as social scientists. They have interests in the definitions, assumptions, arguments, and methods of those fields. The book also deals with people whose approach to problem solving has been influenced by their theories. I deal only briefly with the hard sciences, especially in the 1930s and 1940s. I do not touch on the assumptions of "natural dialectics," derived from Marx and Engels, and having special relevance to physics in the post-Mao period. This is because the assumptions of natural dialectics play no significant role in the early and most recent works by the theorists who serve as my sources.[4] In any case, the spectrum of political, philosophical, and psychological players with whom I deal believed that their findings were applicable to the method of inquiry in all fields where there are human problems. My interest is in the theory and practice of inquiry as a broad human issue, before, during, and after the 1980s.

The subtheme that people operate on different levels at the same time also runs through the chapters that follow. It is appealing to think that people's motives are simple. Many like to say that people are selfish, that their only motive is to maximize their self-interest. My conclusion, after trying to figure out the motives of others, as well as my own, is that our motives are complex and mixed, and rarely only singular. Supposing that I have a bad meal and a rude waiter at a local restaurant. I wish to heave a brick through the restaurant's window. When I ask myself why I do not, I find I have several motives simultaneously. One is clearly self-interested: I do not want to go to jail or pay a fine. But there is another that is equally strong. I do not want to live in a community where people resolve disputes with bricks. My other motive, then, is to show that I respect the law, that I agree with it.

People can shift from one level or motive to another. I apply this principle to twentieth-century China. I show how many important figures were motivated by a desire to act consistently with social values associated with the premodern/received view of knowledge and inquiry. These values included maintaining hierarchies, nurturing the completion of natural purposes, and observing correct relationships. At the same time, these people often had other motives and acted according to them, instead. Sometimes we can identify them, though sometimes they are fairly well concealed. For example, in addition to traditional social values, a person may also believe in utilitarian values and favor actions that support efficiency or entrepreneurship. He also may be motivated by a desire to retain power, or by fear. There are many examples of this in the pages ahead.

Although the chapters that follow refer to the desire to conform to positions associated with a dominant school of thought, such as Zhu Xi or Wang Yangming Neo-Confucianism, or Maoism, such references are not meant to imply that these positions are the only ones. Many competing positions coexist, and the same person can buy into one or the others depending on the circumstances.

What follows is a study of the road to modern problem solving in China. The study points to the tension between a traditional Confucian style of investigation and that associated with science. I argue for differentiating the subjective realm of human values and the realm of nature. I argue for the positive, instrumental role of individual autonomy in Chinese inquiry. I am optimistic about the possibility of such changes taking shape because, as I demonstrate, their seeds are already present in China. They coexist with other, older approaches and are beginning to compete with them in both scholarly and popular culture.

Acknowledgments

This book represents a summing up, towards the end of my active university life, of a few hypotheses I have formed about threads that connect old and new China. Though I cannot deny a certain sense of freedom to plunge into deep thoughts and soar across broad vistas, I have tried to anchor these flights firmly in research that I began back in 1989.

As at any stage in my professional life, I am mindful of debts to many people, students as well as colleagues. If the hypotheses or interpretations have extended beyond reason, that is my doing and not theirs. I am grateful to members of the Department of Philosophy at Peking University, where I did research for parts of this project in 1990. They welcomed me as a Visiting Researcher, facilitated my access to texts, and, through discussions, helped clarify my understanding of Chinese philosophy of the 1930s and 1940s. The Committee on Scholarly Communication with the People's Republic of China of the National Academy of Sciences, generously provided the funding that made possible this stay at Peking University. I also owe a debt to my student and friend, An Yanming. He was able to track down numerous useful materials relevant to the topics with which I deal. A careful reader of portions of the book, he has made helpful suggestions about filling gaps and refining points of emphasis. I am grateful for his contribution to the sense of exhilaration I have when discussing and writing about the topics. My colleague and former student, Lo Yuet-keung, taught me much that I did not know about Xiong Shili.

My sister, Eleanor Munro, is an artist as a writer, where I merely write. She has tried to teach me the difference between strong words and weak words, between saying something simply and clearly and saying it in a clumsy manner. I envy her artistry. I try to learn.

Some long time colleagues and friends read this manuscript in various stages and made such profound critical comments that I had to go back to work, to revise and add. These include Michel Oksenberg, from whom I have learned more than from anyone else the need to look at the same issues not just from a philosophical perspective but also from that of the political scientist. He has helped me in my journey to understanding that, because people operate on different levels, different levels of analysis are necessary to comprehend their acts. Kenneth

Lieberthal has the most detailed knowledge of contemporary China that I have ever encountered. Thank goodness, because he found errors in my accounts of some recent historical events of which I would have been unaware until the grave. As always, I learned fairness and balance in evaluation from Albert Feuerwerker; I added many pages to the first chapter as a result of his suggestions. David Rolston worked with me to formulate a more appropriate title for the book as a whole and for some chapters. He also used the red pen to which he is entitled as Director of Publications, to flag places in the manuscript that needed attention. My friend of long standing, Roger Ames, aimed his critical philosophical arrows at appropriate targets. In important cases he was on the mark. My new friend, William Rowe, gave parts of the manuscript, especially the first chapter, the kind of rigorous reading I had expected of him, because he has the historian's grasp that I will never have. I spent a lot of time changing things as a result and benefited greatly from his reading. During the years that I have worked on the topic of this book, I have often consulted my Philosophy colleague, Peter Railton. He has been unfailingly generous in sharing book references and his own ideas, especially on the matter of epistemic values. Most recently, he helped me understand the instrumental role of investigators' individual autonomy in the social process of inquiry. I am very grateful to him.

Finally, I want to thank the College of Literature, Science, and the Arts at the University of Michigan, which sponsored the Distinguished Senior Faculty Lectures from which this book derives. My daughter Sarah first read my notes for those lectures and suggested where I could take things out and where I could make more sense. So I conclude by admitting that I am at the point where increasingly I learn from my daughter. There is a message there.

The Imperial Style of Inquiry in Twentieth-Century China

Abbreviations

FBIS	*Foreign Broadcast Information Service*
JJQJ	*Jiang Jieshi quanji* 蔣介石全集
JPRS	*Joint Publications Research Service*
RMRB	*Renmin Ribao* 人民日報
ZGQN	*Zhongguo qingnian* 中國青年
ZJXSP	*Zichan jieji xueshu sixiang pipan cankao ziliao* 資產階級學術思想批判參考資料
ZLHB	*Zhongguo xiandai zhexue shi ziliao huibian* 中國現代哲學史資料匯編
ZLHBXJ	*Zhongguo xiandai zhexue shi ziliao huibian xuji* 中國現代哲學史資料匯編續集
ZXZJC	*Zhongguo xiandai zhexueshi jiaoxue cailiao xuanji* 中國現代哲學史教學料選輯

Citations from Chinese collections follow the convention: set (集), volume (册) (in Roman numerals), and page number (頁). Full citations of these collections are given in Works Cited.

CHAPTER ONE

The Imperial Style of Inquiry

Among the founding premises of Chinese civilization was a noble but, in recent centuries, increasingly unworkable idea. It was a version of the not uncommon notion that everything in the universe is part of a coherent, internally structured totality. Events in one part affect another. This idea helped to justify empire and centralized authority in the hands of the emperor, who kept the whole harmonious. I consider it to be noble because it is aesthetically pleasing to our sense of order. It may motivate some people to care for the earth' s resources. It may reassure them that what they think and do can have an impact on the world.

This totalism was associated with views about knowledge and the investigation of things. There were three links between totalism and a certain style of inquiry. First, inquiry was to be guided by models, the legitimacy of which lay in the emperor's approval of them. He served as the ultimate authority on standards for understanding the whole. Second, inquiry should be guided by principles derived from the totalistic portrait of the world: it should recognize that there are hierarchical relations between the parts, noting that parts have purposes and helping them realize their purposes is to the good of the whole; it should maintain the original harmony and vitality among all parts; and it should integrate knowledge of the parts because that knowledge is interrelated. Third, inherent in the human mind are duplicates of the orderly structure or patterns of nature as a whole, so clarifying the mind is the best route toward understanding phenomena in the natural world.

In Praise of China's Totalism

There were many cultural strengths that derived ultimate justification from this totalism. I want to flag them at the start, because this book focuses not on strengths but on an inherent weakness that coexists with them. I do not want to give the impression that the founding premise of the worldview with which I will deal was all bad. The damaging consequences of its weakness did not come to the fore until the past two centuries or so, though that weakness was certainly manifest earlier. Prior to the nineteenth century, the strengths occupied the foreground. But historical conditions changed, eroding those strengths and thereby making society more vulnerable to the damage that could be done by the weakness. I will identify a number of strengths and in each case conclude by explaining how it was undercut eventually by historical developments.

The biggest historical change was in the self-confidence among elite Chinese about their place in what constitutes "the world" (*tianxia*). Prior to the nineteenth century, in both theory and experience, the world was the Chinese cultural world. Chinese relations with tributary countries and peoples, from the northern nomads and Tibetans to the West, to the Vietnamese and Koreans, were consistent with this view. Generally, their emissaries came as tribute-bearing subordinates to the Chinese emperor. (There are some examples of Chinese flexibility in foreign policy, when certain foreigners were treated as equals). Even when ethnically non-Chinese, the rulers of China assimilated Chinese culture. Within this culture, the emperor of China was the key to relations between all humans and heaven. This is part of the totalistic perspective. But after the end of the eighteenth century, the idea and the experience of what constitutes the world began to shift. The cause was China' s increasing relations with a bigger and different world. In this new realm of relations, other monarchs had competing claims and the arms to back them up. The English kings and queens were among the chief players in these new relations. As a result of the successes in China of monarchs from outside of the Chinese cultural realm, among which the Opium War (1839–41) looms large, it gradually became impossible for Chinese elites to sustain their confidence in the old ideas about the world. The world was no longer coextensive with Chinese culture, and the Chinese ruler was no longer the obvious sole middleman between humans and heaven. The totalistic political view began to erode.

The strengths that derived from the totalistic vision were particularly evident in Chinese society during the centuries before the shift away from that vision began. The first strength lay in the idea that the totality incorporating humans and nature was stabilized and secured by a single ruler with special responsibilities. This ruler represented the people to heaven (nature) and heaven to the people. The relationship was conceived on the family analogy. The ruler was Son-of-Heaven and father of the people. With this role came responsibilities, originally identified by the Confucian philosopher Mencius (372?–279? B.C.), to look after the economic and educational well-being of the population. As a parent nurtures children or as a gardener cultivates her plants, the ruler must look after the welfare of the people to whom he is tied in this structured totality. At the very least, this meant insuring that state granaries were able to provide food for them in times of famine and stabilizing the flow of food and other commodities to the regional markets. It meant appointing officials who could also serve as exemplars for the moral education of the people. The reciprocal obligation of "children" was obedience.

In addition to the role of economic variables, such as pressure on resources from population growth, this system began to break down because of the weakening of the central government as it dealt with foreign incursions and internal rebellions in the nineteenth century. In addition, starting with the Sino-Japanese War of 1894–95, increasing numbers of educated elite wanted to participate in their own governance. Gradually, modern Chinese nationalism emerged. Many educated people reacted favorably to teachings about Western democracy that had been around for decades in translation and later were given new content in the writings of returned students, such as Dr. Hu Shi (1891–1962). They were also attracted to certain elements in their own New Text School, of which Kang Youwei (1857–1927), was the most famous proponent, and in the Statecraft (*jingshi*) tradition. These emphasized changing society by making fundamental changes in established institutions. They prized the individual Confucian official as reformer, and took the Han ideologue and official Dong Zhongshu (179?–104? B.C.) and the early seventeenth century Donglin academicians as models. This helped to undermine the ability of central authority to perform its traditional nurturing tasks.

A second strength lay in the family ethic and the communitarian values associated with it. The totalistic universe was one in which nature, the state, and the community all could and should exemplify certain traits, some of which were readily identified with the family: role relationships, hierarchy, and reciprocal responsibilities. Psychologically, there is much in the Confucian claim that knowledge and sentiments about morality are derived from the universal parent-child relationship. The family often provided a reliable source of support for the individual at the community level by giving him a known network of responsible connections. This ethic promoted order in the broader community by laying out a set of social roles analogous to those in a family for all persons. This made behavior predictable to some degree and was reinforced as patriarchal community figures resolved conflicts in ways that took account of those roles.

At the same time, the structure of role relations was flexible enough to accommodate those outside one's own family or community. Chinese merchants often used adaptations of familiar Chinese instruments to aid in the transition to international commercial procedures. These were built into the Chinese-controlled distribution system for goods, regularized over centuries by merchants well used to moving around their own country and to dealing with people outside of their normal networks.

However, the reliance on family rules and relationships in dealing with problems began to lose its effectiveness when, in the nineteenth and early twentieth centuries, Chinese people were increasingly involved in economic transactions governed by procedures not familiar to them, and political conditions changed. One of the most famous examples is the experience of the Standard Oil Company, which around 1900 got into the business of selling kerosene for home lighting from its headquarters in Shanghai to local Chinese wholesale distributors in rural areas. The rural wholesalers lived in a different social world from that of the American managers and their Chinese aides in the home office in Shanghai. The procedures affected by changing conditions included the pricing of kerosene by the home office without local flexibility, and granting private credit. In the case of credit, in the early years of the company's business dealings, family members of Chinese agents accepted responsibility for repayment. Avoiding clan shame for default was a high priority. Later, with the emergence of unstable warlord governments, those family responsibilities eroded. Debts were not repaid and the foundation of private credit evaporated.[1] A need arose for state-enforced institutions, such as civil laws governing banking and new rules about contracts. These are universal in application and normally do not take account of role relationships. These institutions have remained relatively undeveloped in China in the twentieth century.

The prizing of education was the third strength derived from the totalistic worldview. In part it followed from the ruler' s obligation to nurture his "children." It also came from the belief that the principles of all categories of things already exist in each person' s mind. Education was the means by which people learned to gain access to them. On the practical side, education was also the means whereby the state trained civil servants to run the government. Their ordering capability was largely dependent on their understanding of those principles. Education and privilege went together. Thus, the Chinese state attracted many talented people into its service through its schools and its civil service examinations. Further, they learned in the schools a perspective and a set of social values shared by most members of their class. This fostered efficiency in handling affairs.

An edict of 1044 ordered each prefecture and county with a minimum number of scholars in it to set up schools. By the end of the Northern Song in 1125 there were 200,000 students in government schools. Though popular education did not take off for another three centuries, this marked the beginning of state-sponsored education on a considerable scale. The genuine interest in rewarding educational achievement with privilege is revealed by attempts to exercise objectivity in evaluating the civil service examinations. In the case of the palace, or highest level, examinations in 992, the names of candidates written on examination papers were covered over, and in 1015 it was ordered that the papers be rewritten, so authorship could not be inferred from knowledge of a candidate' s calligraphy. Over time various regions came to be important contributors of successful candidates. These educated elites had access to literature and to persons with a range of styles and experiences in problem solving, though they had been indoctrinated to favor mainly one. In short, offices were staffed from a pool of talented and accomplished individuals who were well-equipped to handle the problems of governing.

However, by the end of the Qing dynasty, the number of qualified people was inadequate to deal with the range of problems facing the state, centrally or locally. In part this was because the state was parsimonious in spending money on bureaucratic salaries. In the Qing, out of a total population of two hundred million, there were five million active and former candidates for the lowest civil service degree, but only 27,000 office holders. In part this inadequate quantity of office holders reflects more than an unwillingness to spend money on appointments. It was also a consequence of the concern with ideological orthodoxy. The elite graduates of schools and successful examination candidates shared values. If such sharing had the virtue of promoting cohesion, in the late Qing it also obstructed the state' s fostering of new technical skills and providing employment for those who possessed them. Those skills might have been promoted through a new curriculum. The state also was set on obstructing consideration of newly introduced Western values, such as toleration of plurality of beliefs and objectivity in investigation. There were some signs of change from the top in 1898 when the provincial governor Zhang Zhidong (1837–1909) instituted educational reforms leading to the teaching of sciences in the Western manner. But without strong state support, the quantity of graduates trained in the new ways of technical problem solving remained inadequate.

Fourth and finally, the kind of education promoted by the state fostered a self-discipline that gave great strength to many of those entrusted with public service. It emphasized intuitive self-knowledge, because it is within the mind that one finds the principles of the integrated totalistic whole and the controllable selfish desires that obscure them. This education also emphasized the role of models in learning. In defense of the Confucian position, I would say that in character development, model emulation is highly effective. It prizes moral spontaneity as the highest trait of the sage, quite distinct from the Western concern with rational choice-making from among alternatives. In situations requiring ethical action, to be able to do the right thing spontaneously is a virtue. This approach helped nurture great heroes, such as Wang Yangming (1472–1529). His discipline gave him the courage to send a memorial to the throne in 1506 that led to his being flogged until he lost consciousness. It helped him find meaning in his years of banishment to remote Guizhou province, which he spent educating the local populace.

However, beliefs that exalt a mind supposedly already in possession of totalistic knowledge obstruct acquaintance with any new kind of knowledge. This sort of knowledge was being generated in Western Europe in the eighteenth and nineteenth centuries and began to trickle into China. What was needed was a complete shift in orientation about the nature of inquiry and state support for that shift. Exploring the need for this shift and uncovering the opportunities for its occurrence are the focus of the remainder of this work.

Critical Weaknesses

Over the past century of social change, Western observers and the rare Chinese pioneer have realized that there are problems with the psychological premise of the old totalistic idea. It fails to free the mind to evaluate the world accurately in a time of peril. The mind is not free, according to the totalistic worldview; its content is already fixed; its structure contains the orderly patterns of the outer world.

Humans and nature share traits. According to this old concept, they share purposive action toward goals (nature' s purposes include the production of life), hierarchy (the pole star is superior to other stars that do homage to it), consistency within patterns of process, role fulfillment, and reciprocal relations (between persons, between mountains, and other things). All these not only exist in the world but also are innately part of the mind. If you understand the human mind, you understand nature. If you control the mind, you can control the outer world. This is because things in the world fit into categories that we discriminate with language. Their goals, hierarchical ranks, roles, and relations vary as a function of their categories. The mind' s endowment includes knowledge of these categories. When the mind causes our actions to accord with the relevant categories in the world, those actions are auspicious. They succeed.

The doctrine of a structured totality supports a style of inquiry focusing on the triumphant abilities of the mind. "Style of inquiry" refers to both a way of interpreting problems and arriving at possible solutions to them. Conforming to a style of inquiry is the way the mind controls things. I will refer to Chinese inquiry as the "imperial style of inquiry," which is based on Neo-Confucian orthodoxy. This expression is meant to highlight the political nature of inquiry and its role in orthodox education and government examinations (from 1313 to 1905). These dates indicate how long this style of inquiry has been around and suggest that the civil service exam and schools were the institutional means of enforcing its practice. To call it the imperial style also emphasizes the fact that most people had to give nominal assent to it, even if in their behavior they ignored it. This does not mean that its adherents over the centuries all have had government affiliations. Many who subscribed to this style of inquiry had no interest in government service.

The imperial style involved three interrelated beliefs. First, a condition of success in investigating and solving a problem is the willpower of a mind that is clear about and committed to acting in accord with the innate traits just mentioned—moral purpose, hierarchy, and consistency. Such a clarified mind is said to be "rectified." Second (and related to the first), emulating models is the best way for most people to learn these traits and to clear and rectify their minds. The cloudy condition that afflicts most minds usually disappears with the concentrated study of models—actual, or as portrayed in texts. Third, only a limited number of things are worth knowing. The traits shared by humans and nature, discovered through intuition or from models, effectively define the limits of inquiry. To narrow the scope even more, relationships, especially hierarchical human relationships, are the subjects most worthy of study.

These beliefs about inquiry often go together. Modern social scientists and philosophers writing about China have referred to the first as voluntarism (Latin *voluntas*, for will, as in willpower.) This technical term is a bit like the English expression "mind [willpower] over matter." By extension, I may sometimes refer to all three beliefs as "Chinese voluntarism," using the term in a unique way to refer to the interrelated components of this style of inquiry. But by and large I will try to avoid the term, because English readers may wrongly think of "volunteerism" rather than of mind over matter when they see the word voluntarism.

These core beliefs have shaped Chinese philosophy, scholarly essays, and political practice from the Song period (960–1279) to the present. However, we do not find the concept of totalistic structure or this style of inquiry among all Chinese. It may be identified with certain groups of elites. For example, Confucian thinkers are famous for believing that morally correct ideas in people' s minds are the necessary and sometimes even the sufficient condition for practical success in dealing with concrete problems.

Ideas about a totalistic world and about the style of inquiry derived from it divert attention from a detailed examination of empirical facts in any objective situation. The first of the core beliefs suggests that a clarified and rectified mind is more important than any objective factor that resolution of a problem situation might involve, such as technical skills, machinery, raw materials, or physical terrain. Model emulation diverts attention from the unique features of a situation to a model that may or may not fit that situation. The third view, that there is a limited number of things worth investigating, tends to cause any investigation to refocus on one of those things shared by humans and nature to the exclusion of the original subject. For example, a scientific topic will turn into a study of the social relationships of the investigators.

The explanation for the endurance of this elite perspective into the twentieth century lies with received views about the nature of learning and the nature of knowledge originating in the teachings of Zhu Xi and Wang Yangming. These teachings have been widely studied in the school curriculum in the centuries since these men wrote them. They encourage concern with the mind (and for Zhu Xi, with texts) and discourage broad or detailed concern with objective facts.

Ideas about the proper style of inquiry cut across many of the elite' s professions, from political leaders to academics. Modern elites of all political persuasions have suffered from its limitations. It has reappeared since the 1911 revolution, and it endures even now at the end of the century.

The persistence and broad embrace of this style will be news to some people. When they think of confidence in the power of the will, of reliance on models, and of a politically determined narrow scope of inquiry, they will remember Chairman Mao. He was the one singled out by foreign analysts and by Chinese critics after his death as distinctive for accentuating the politically correct will in several of his policies. The Great Leap Forward and the communes of the 1950s were said to involve politicized willpower as answers to China' s industrial backwardness and to the family-oriented farming practices and purely local outlook of China' s peasants. The Cultural Revolution of the 1960s was Mao' s mind-transforming answer to threats to his egalitarian plans for Chinese society and to his own power from within the party. These three policies have been treated as proof of his inheritance of that style. They are proof of its high cost to the Chinese people as well. Most people, however, believe that these policies were simply Mao' s quirks, which he foisted on his officials. Those officials then proceeded to drum his style of analysis into everyone' s head via books, speeches, and campaigns. Those living at the end of the century still remember that, mercifully, once Mao died, people could begin to undo the damage that resulted from his perspective on willpower.

But this picture is wrong. It is wrong because it fails to treat Mao' s premises as those of the elite in general, shared by his non-Communist predecessors and enduring after his death even among reform-minded dissidents. Vast numbers of elites have inherited and continue to pass on those premodern ideas about inquiry.

Totalism, East and West

The Confucian style of inquiry is associated with the holistic portrait of the universe, because the traits in nature worth studying are also found in the mind. As early as the Warring States period, over two thousand years ago, and as recently as the 1930s, the phrase "the unity of heaven and humans" has been used to describe this integrated totality. In the Northern Song dynasty (960-1126), the name for the orderly pattern of the universe was *taiji* (great ultimate). In one sense, the unity of heaven and humans refers to the sharing of traits described above. The Neo-Confucians, who began to flourish in the eleventh century, overcame any dualism between heaven and humans by resorting to a macrocosm-microcosm idea borrowed from the Buddhists (the Buddha is present in each thing in its entirety). This shaped the Confucian claim that *taiji*, or the structure of the universe and its classes of things, is present in the mind of each person. If the structure of nature exhibits certain traits, those traits are also in the mind.

In another sense, this idea of unity means that there is no separating the two realms that we identify as subjective or private and objective or public. This does not mean that the difference was not understood. Zhu Xi sometimes used the terms *nei* (inner) and *wai* (outer) to refer to inner feelings and outer conduct. Many writers enjoined people to be sure that their outer conduct corresponded to their inner sentiments, avoiding hypocrisy. However, these were not the fundamental categories used for talking about humans in their environment.

The terminology that points to the unity of people and their environment describes a processional dualism rather than a duality of type. Its central terms are *ti* (potentiality/quietude) and *yong* (actualization/movement). This pairing avoids a dualism between the mental and the external because it places both psychological activity and overt conduct under the umbrella of actualization/movement. What Westerners call private (beliefs, desires), the Neo-Confucians treated as forms of movement on their way to overt appearance. The bottom line is that in moving, the mind participates in the same activity as all natural objects. The same explanatory language applies to both mind and objects.

If a dualism of the knowing mind and external things is avoided by asserting that both have the same traits, there is also a psychological means for accomplishing this anti-dualist end. This is accomplished by encouraging the investigator to establish an empathic relation with what he investigates. The sympathetic relations reinforce the belief that the person lives in a non-alienating world.[2]

These are not the only reasons Confucianism seeks to avoid dualism. Even an outside analyst can recognize that, from a political standpoint, placing humans and nature under the same umbrella shores up the legitimacy of the state in controlling everything within its reach and power. It also elevates the power and stature of those who say they understand the patterns of nature. Those who claim to know the patterns, believing that in uniformity lies stability, can demand uniformity of behavior from subjects on the grounds that such behavior is "natural." Because the emperor is the Son-of-Heaven, his mind is the supreme living embodiment of heavenly traits. This makes him the supreme model to emulate. Imitate heaven by copying the emperor.

This Confucian holism is not without its counterparts in the West. Well into the nineteenth century, Chinese and Western holisms shared certain features. First, human traits, such as consciousness and purposiveness, are attributed to some whole; second, a person, and especially a person' s mind, can only be understood in terms of his relation to some whole, such as the family, *dao*, society, or *taiji*, in the Chinese case, or God and community in the Western case. One cannot give a complete account of a person simply by referring to his individual emotions, interests, talents, or unique characteristics, or give an account of his mind simply by referring to the objective stimuli that impinge on it. Finally, insofar as wholes have purposes, the destiny of any individual thing or person depends on its relation to the whole and its purposes. A critical purpose of the Confucian whole, for instance, was the reproduction of life. Relevant Chinese technical terms for this include *mudi lun* (teleology) and *qu* (the notion of having a natural tendency in a certain direction).

Teleological explanations of the natural and social worlds dominated in the West under Aristotelian influence until the sixteenth century. The geocentric universe, with the human world at the center, is part of that portrait. It also assumes that each of the four elements (earth, water, air, fire) has its own natural position (akin to the Chinese idea of *fen*, or allotted place, within a whole). Things have their purposes and potentialities, which unfold within the natural order.

Plato described the world as "a living organism with soul and reason,"[3] and the organism has remained a favorite analogy with holistic thinkers. Saint Augustine and others who inherited a form of Platonic holism wrote about the idea of God being innate to the minds of humans, the basic truth from which we deduce other truths. Here we approach the Confucian notion of *taiji* in individual minds. The Platonic legacy claims that the content of individual minds is derivative. Knowledge may derive directly from God, or as in Rousseau' s thinking, it may derive from the community, a whole that possesses the highest moral worth. In any case, the ultimate source of knowledge is something other than the effect of objective stimuli on the individual' s mind. The form of inquiry that was shaped by this premise was associated with a holism that affirmed a linkage between God and minds, or social communities and minds.

Eventually, teleology was thrown out in Europe, in part because it was useless for making the improvements in navigation and artillery demanded by ambitious monarchs and officials of competing countries. Nor could a person use it to advance the understanding of natural phenomena like electricity or gases.[4] New intellectual developments contributed as much as broad historical movements to the gradual shift from teleology in the West. Copernicus' heliocentric view represents a milestone in thinking about the universe. However, his theory was rejected by many for reasons of religious dogma and by others because it seemed plain that the Earth does not move. Descartes' doctrine that the world of nature has only quantifiable characteristics–extension and motion–was also an individual milestone. Purpose is excluded from nature. Of course, the habit of reading moral purpose into nature continued long after these intellectual watersheds, and a number of teleologically inclined observers also made discoveries that advanced knowledge about the world. Darwin' s work, however, finally knocked Western teleology from professional intellectual circles in the second part of the nineteenth century. Stephen Jay Gould puts it this way:

> This tradition of attempting to read moral meaning from nature did not cease with the triumph of evolutionary theory in 1859--for evolution could be read as God' s chosen method to people our planet, and ethical messages might still populate nature. . . . It took Darwin himself to derail this ancient tradition. . . .[5]

Another hero in the shift from teleological thinking was Galileo. He was the first to design a mathematical model of a certain world and then to construct experiments to test whether or not the world he lived in corresponded to it. In the words of A. C. Crombie:

> It may be argued that it was, above all, Galileo who showed how to disembarrass nature of its moral charge, and who through his public controver-

sies and their consequences focused the moral enterprise of science instead as one of inalienable freedom of responsible inquiring minds to search for objective truth.[6]

A Confucian scholar might describe Galileo' s enterprise as separating humans and heaven, or dividing the moral mind from nature. From Galileo' s perspective, however, this separation enables us to study nature without regard to the moral traits that political or religious figures might claim it possesses.

Defining the West's New Paradigm

"Scientific method" is the term we usually apply to the style of inquiry that arose in the West, in part in opposition to the style of deduction from self-evident truths associated with the holistic metaphysics. It leaves Aristotle and Plato behind, along with the attribution of human social values to nature. The classic study of scientific method for beginners in the United States starts like this:

> The method of science does not seek to impose the desires and hopes of men upon the flux of things in a capricious manner. It may indeed be employed to satisfy the desires of men. But its successful use depends upon seeking, in a deliberate manner, and irrespective of what men' s desires are, to recognize, as well as to take advantage of, the structure which the flux possesses.[7]

In speaking about styles of inquiry I will use the expression "to drive inquiry." This points to the idea that something guides the investigator' s progress in solving what he has identified as a problem. The scientific method insists that this guiding should be done by hypotheses and by newly discovered facts, facts which may change continually. The crucial point here is that there can be no antecedently relevant facts as there would be if there were a moral or officially sanctioned model that could be imposed on a problem being studied. Morris R. Cohen and Ernest Nagel, the authors of that classic introduction to scientific method, stated,

> Consequently what the ' facts' are must be determined by inquiry, and cannot be determined antecedently to inquiry. . . . There is therefore no sharp line dividing facts from guesses or hypotheses. During any inquiry the status of a proposition may change from that of hypothesis to that of fact, or from that of fact to that of hypothesis.[8]

So inquiry is driven as much by facts as by educated guesses. And the reference is to facts as interpreted by the individual or group of individuals doing the investigating. This is a method that is self-correcting. There is no external authority whose position is final and may intrude on the investigators. There are no innate first principles. No verification of a hypothesis is more than approximate.

Needless to say, there were metaphysical precedents for the principles of the "scientific method." That method holds investigators as the immediate authority, and their research possesses an authority not mediated by a priori ideas or by the community (save that hypotheses must not contradict too many prior beliefs). The precedents for this lie in opposition to the totalistic structure of the Aristotelian and Platonic traditions that unite human values and natural traits.

As Chad Hansen has noted, it became a goal of the so-called atomistic individualists, such as Hobbes and Locke, to lead a type of revolt against holism in Europe.[9] Their position was that each individual is an independent source of knowledge, and that individuals are autonomous in what they do with that knowledge. We get our information in private experience, unmediated by God or social community. Locke was most prominent in working out the political implications of this thesis. He justified the value of individual autonomy that forms part of liberal individualism. His thesis also helps to justify the value of freedom of conscience: my beliefs are my private business, and I am the best judge of the conclusions I draw from my experience.

In the second half of this book I will describe modern Chinese arguments for the individual acquiring information without the mediation of a heavenly or secular authority. Chapter 4 outlines the movement to separate the realms of heaven and humans, thereby undercutting any possible claims about the heavenly derived content of the mind. This separation clearly disjoins the traits of the mind from the traits of nature (heaven) or objects. Among other things, chapter 5 will compare the historical contexts in which certain influential Westerners and Chinese were able to reject the authority of theological or political control over the content of mind. My point is to show that there have been historical circumstances that have bolstered a shift in metaphysical and epistemological paradigms. This was true in Europe and has been true in China since at least the 1930s.

Chinese Styles of Inquiry

Origins of Imperial Confucian Inquiry

The style of inquiry discussed by Confucian thinkers and eventually accepted as state orthodoxy, like that of the Aristotelians and Platonists in the West, derived from a conception of a totalistic universe. It was a style of inquiry that filtered out facts not relevant to moral purpose, hierarchy, and consistency with inherent patterns shared by humans and nature. For most people it emphasized model emulation as a means to clarify the mind' s grasp of the patterns of heaven, the emperor' s ultimate model. It also directed introspection about the structure of nature for the highly educated. It was optimistic about the consequences of controlling the mind: The key to understanding nature is to understand the mind. This is because it is the most readily accessible thing that a human has ("...a man who knows his own nature will know heaven," said Mencius).[10] Because heavenly traits are imprinted on the mind, the person with a clarified or rectified mind, knowing the traits, can make his actions coincide with the natural patterns. Success follows. Exploring the origins of this intellectual tradition will illuminate the degree to which it is tied to a totalistic universe and also its pervasiveness in the history of Chinese thought.

Clearly, the imperial style of inquiry owes something to the Confucian legacy symbolized by an eight step sequence mapped out in the third century B.C. essay, *The Great Learning*. This essay states that there is an inevitable progression from having a rectified mind to achieving success both in running a household and in governing a country. Indeed, a rectified mind is a necessary condition of practical success. The Warring States Confucians also contributed the claim that virtuous character, manifest in benevolent action, contains the seed of strength, in spite of military or economic weakness. Mencius makes the following point to one of the kings of those warring states:

> If your majesty practises benevolent government towards the people, reduces punishment and taxation, gets people to plough deeply and weed promptly,...then they can be made to inflict defeat on the strong armour and sharp weapons of Ch'in and Ch'u, armed with nothing but staves.[11]

A virtuous but weak king will triumph because the people in neighboring states will defect to him, turning over their weapons. The previously strong king will become weak:

> With the people of other states growing daily more eager to fight against him, and his own people growing daily less eager to fight in his defense, the ruler who relies upon strength will on the contrary be reduced to weakness.[12]

This idea was reinforced by the law of reversal of opposites (from weakness to strength) found in the Daoist text *Laozi*: "That the weak overcomes the strong, / And the submissive overcomes the hard, / Everyone in the world knows, yet no one can put this knowledge into practice."[13] This means that few people understand that aggressive bullies often end up dead while the nonassertive survive.

Song and Ming dynasty Neo-Confucians are the immediate source of the claim, still vibrant in our century, that actions emanating from the intuitive moral sense are always appropriate to their external situations. This was called the *dao*-mind or *liangzhi* (innate moral knowledge). We can all cultivate our *dao*-minds (Zhu Xi) or commit ourselves to be sincere about our *liangzhi* (Wang Yangming). Then, mirror-like, our *dao*-minds will reflect everything that is important in a situation, no matter how circumstances change over time. Actions continually meet the needs of the moment and there is a unity of knowledge and action. Wang Yangming used these words, "The mind of the sage is like a clear mirror. Since it is all clarity, it responds to all stimuli as they come and reflects everything."[14]

Another idea with Song-Ming roots is moral spontaneity, to which I have already alluded. Originally, in Confucianism this referred to the fact that it is possible to train oneself to act in accordance with the ritual rules of conduct all the time. The end of this long process of socialization is a condition in which what one desires to do and the "right" (consistent with the ritual rules recorded in the classic texts) thing to do are automatically the same. The *Analects* reports that Confucius attained this condition at the age of seventy.[15] The important point is that there is a crucial trait of the Cheng-Zhu school and Wang Yangming sagely ideal that overlaps to some degree with a trait in the Daoist sage. It is captured in the idea of spontaneity. A sage disdains analytical thought, the evaluation of reasons, and rational choice-making, in clear contrast to the Western cultural hero who is valued precisely for his ability to reason. By Song-Ming times, the moral spontaneity of the sage also disdained purposiveness. As described in the texts of these schools, the sage was a person whose mind was so finely honed that he had no need to think *or* plan. His actions were automatically correct responses to objective circumstances. As Wang Yangming said,

> Principle involves no activity. Always to know, to preserve, and to regard principle as fundamental means not to see, hear, think, or act [deliberately]. Not to do these things does not mean to be like dry wood or dead ashes. When one sees, hears, thinks, and acts in complete accord with principle and makes no deliberate effort to do so, it means [sic] activity and at the same time no activity.[16]

Significantly, there was an alternative tradition within Confucianism that treated the sage as a careful field administrator, alert to the empirical conditions involved in solving specific problems. This was the Statecraft legacy of Confucians who took seriously the need to study and analyze problems in cartography (for military maps) and hydraulics (for flood control), among other subjects. Statecraft thinkers were especially influential in the Qing period and profoundly influenced the New Text thinkers.

The older idea that practical success comes from having a rectified or moral mind lingered into the early twentieth century when it met with other, foreign ones. The latter contained the little-known European seeds of the later Chinese vision of "permanent revolution."[17] This is a fancy term for a type of voluntarism. In a nutshell, this doctrine held that an elite of "proletarian" revolutionaries armed with the right ideas (consciousness) can take over the bourgeois revolution and rapidly telescope the development of a modern industrial economy and the emergence of socialist persons, in spite of the actual underdevelopment of a country. As John Plamenetz noted long ago, this doctrine appeared in an earlier form in Marx' s *Address to the Communist League* (1850) and in Lenin' s "Two Tactics of Social Democracy in the Democratic Revolution."[18] Li Dazhao (1888–1927) served as a bridge in the transmission of these ideas to Mao. Li emphasized the positive role proletarian class consciousness could play in the modernization of China. He treated such consciousness as something both generated by class struggle and also as already shared to some degree by most Chinese because of their experiences with imperialist powers. While the concept of class consciousness came from Marx, the possibility of its cultivation in preindustrial China, which lacked Marx' s prerequisite economic conditions, was highlighted by Li and favored by Mao.

Thus, unlike much modern Chinese thinking on this topic, Maoist beliefs about the power of the mind contain a good dose of foreign ingredients as well as Confucian and Daoist ones. The new dress in which Mao cloaked the Confucian roots of his thinking was the assertion that humans have malleable social natures (thought, beliefs, attitudes) and less malleable biological natures (innate abilities, survival needs). In coping successfully with any problem, what matters most is the condition of the former and not the latter.

The Process of Confucian Inquiry

Models and Inquiry

The process begins with a belief in model emulation, because this is often the means by which ordinary people rectify their minds, creating the condition whereby their willpower will prevail over possible objective constraints. There is a substantial amount of early Chinese writing on the theory and practice of model emulation. Much of it reveals acute psychological insights valid in any culture and any historical era. This applies especially to the usefulness of models in the socialization of children. Educational texts and historical writings are filled with positive and negative models. Chinese educators know that children learn ethical practices or consciousness of a moral sense in large part through what Westerners call "observational learning" from adults. Models are also useful in the transmission of technical skills in the workplace.

However, in terms of the goal of promoting objective inquiry, the reliance on models has resulted in a certain dysfunction in China. An important contributor to that dysfunction has been the use of officially sanctioned models for the political goal of making people easier to govern or "order." Models have become a tool for ensuring uniformity of thought and eliminating individual or nonorthodox taste and judgment. This is the kind of model with which I am concerned in this study.

Most generally, the individual emulates the mind or attitude or character traits of this kind of model. These models enforce uniformity of thought because all people are taught to emulate the minds of the same models. As political leaders see it, this uniformity makes people' s behavior (and expectations) predictable and society stable. Common traditional expressions to describe this uniformity are *da yitong* (grand unity of everything), which refers to the existence of uniform standards for all thoughts and actions, and *yixin* (one-mindedness). The same standard might permit different duties and punishments or rewards because of role differences. Uniformity in practice is often measured by whether or not an individual' s choice of words is consistent with the standards of orthodoxy, and, of course, by his degree of compliance with official rules.

As with model emulation, one-mindedness may have some positive results. Within an organization or small group, it may promote work discipline where discipline fosters efficiency. It may prevent destructive competitiveness. It is a work style with which Chinese have been comfortable. At the same time, it inhibits criticism of the patriarchal model or his policies.

In discussing the Confucian style of inquiry, the model I am primarily concerned with is a person or persons with certain character traits, or a textual description of such persons. Such a model may exemplify willpower. But more important, the model stands for certain official values and the attitude toward those values that leaders or elites wish people to emulate uniformly. In addition, the model represents intuitive clarity or enlightenment about the structure of nature from which those values derive, an insight shared by only a few people. In order to be prepared to solve practical problems, people should habitually study and imitate what is in the mind and character of a model. In the premodern period the exemplary character traits included social role fulfillment (for example, filiality to parents, loyalty to sovereign). In the modern period, they include obedience to the Party and patriotism. With the focus on general qualities of the model, there is a corresponding disinterest in the specifics of particular situations to which one should apply the model' s ways of thinking and acting.

Here is the justification for seeking a model to emulate. In the words of the Neo-Confucian thinker, Zhu Xi, "We learn the *dao* of the sages so we can know the mind of the sages. When we know the mind of the sages and use that to manage our minds to the point where they are no different from that of the sage, this is what is called the transmission of the mind."[19] The sages knew how to act. By copying their minds, we will know how to act as well. Never mind the details of current problems on which one intends to work.

Problems resulting from this inattention to actual conditions were compounded by an additional interest in models of a different kind: ideal situations described in texts. Often committed to memory, these situational models were considered archetypal of actual cases. Some of these were models of organizations or institutions associated with a morally exemplary utopian age, as is the case with the institutions of the early Zhou regime (founded roughly 1027 B.C.). But these models are themselves general, exemplifying types or categories of situations.

Zhu Xi' s writings reveal several types of these text-based situational models. Most sacred were those laid out in the *Four Books*, starting with *The Great Learning*, and certain commentaries on them by Zhu Xi and others.[20] Other texts containing model institutions and practices were the *Rites of Zhou* (*Zhou li*) and the *Record of Rites* (*Li ji*). Emperors served as models of a correct mind-set, too, when they themselves concentrated on emulating the early sage-kings. Zhu wrote that the emperor was "like a guidepost" while the people were "like its shadow."[21] As such, the ruler promotes uniformity of values. Then there were "true Confucians," who may or may not have had any official capacity. Though wearing the clothes (roles) of commoners, their job was to transform and nurture the people and be models for other literati.[22] Historically, emperors and officials were always setting up local models and erecting arches or other structures to honor them. Even in the case of these models, what counts most is the minds or characters of the participants in the events to which the model supposedly applies.

According to the practice of using models drawn from the *Four Books*, when a problematic event occurred and officials were asked to examine it, their method of inquiry *should* have followed these principles: First, they should identify the appropriate human model for the situation, and they should investigate the attitude of the people involved in the event. All the while, the investigators would encourage the local people to emulate the chosen model' s mind and character traits. This model constituted the standard for evaluating their own attitudes and commitments. Second, the investigation of the event itself should be guided by the textual account of an archetypal event. Attention was shifted away from the objective case and projected instead onto models, onto values in the minds of the participants, and onto preexisting, formulaic textual situations.

From an early time, popular lore reveals that people with morally upright minds had nearly magical control of events. Here is a story dating from a fourth century A.D. collection:

> Xu Xu ...of the Latter Han came from the Youchuan district in Wu. When young he was a prison warder and managed all aspects of his office with great care and fairness. When he was made Magistrate in Xiaohuang, contiguous districts were plagued by great locust swarms which left them as bare as the barrens, but they flew past Xiaohuang and never swarmed there. The Regional Inspector on his round of inspection, however, accused Xu of not governing well. Xu resigned and locusts responded by promptly invading Xiaohuang. The Inspector apologized, Xu Xu returned to his office, and the locusts immediately flew away. [23]

The belief in a relation between rectified minds and practical success became an important part of the Neo-Confucian orthodoxy established in 1313. I will use another example to illustrate how human, textual, and situational models played a role in problem solving. In the late sixteenth century, as Ray Huang has described it, problems faced by the central government included unpaid officials, the absence of money to finance a strong army and a lack of funds to repair dikes for flood control. Huang states,

> Numerous business proceedings that should have been carried out according to organizational principles were actually handled by the personal touch. One of the reasons for this was that, at the outset, the state settled for a level of income too low to finance its operations throughout the immense empire. The salary scale of the Civil Service was set so low that many officials were virtually unpaid.
>
> Although it recognized these undesirable conditions, the court in the later period was helpless to provide a fundamental cure for them. The dynasty had followed the vision of the *Four Books* too closely to consider other approaches. Adjudging simple living a permanent national characteristic, the bureaucratic apparatus had deliberately been constructed to avoid technical complexities. . . . The Civil Service had neither the administrative expertise nor the necessary service facilities to allow itself to keep pace with a national economy that was expanding in both size and degree of sophistication.[24]

The highest official in the bureaucracy in charge of these matters was unable to initiate the tax reforms and land surveys (for tax purposes) to find the money to deal with these matters. The means available to him for solving problems included: using the *Four Books* of Confucianism to provide sagely models of character traits (especially frugality) which he and other senior officials could copy and by means of which they could harmonize invaders and bandits through their own exemplary characters; using those classics as situational models for managing the state; and appointing virtuous (frugal) officials whose exemplary traits would transform the local Chinese people's minds.

There were probably ten different reasons why the person responsible could not get the money, including obstruction by vested interests. But one of them was that his style of inquiry limited him to a list of choices in which options such as these dominated, and he was unable to uncover the objective facts about how much money potentially was available. Tax quotas had not been revised in two hundred years; assessments did not correspond to holdings; rich districts had low tax quotas. The funds could have been extracted, but the official could not get at them. The *Four Books* did not provide a suitable model for the problems of that time, in this case, for financial reform. Unfortunately, the frugality policy was not effective at filling the treasury, driving away invaders or repairing the dikes. Failure to cope with the military and water control problems were two of several factors that weakened the dynasty. By the middle of the next century, it had collapsed.

The traditional Confucian style of inquiry emphasizes models and intuitive or subjective concerns. It encourages an investigator to make sure that commitment to basic values and to problem solving approaches embodied in the model is firm and sincere.

Narrowing the Scope of Knowledge

Officials on the scene may have been adept at gathering information about flooding or markets, but many Confucians have treated knowledge as restricted to morally significant traits supposedly shared by humans and heaven. "Heaven" is a name that, among other things, refers to the orderly patterns in nature. Standards of value are derived from this order. Thus, the scope of what is worth investigating excludes a whole rich range of empirically descriptive facts not pertinent to these concerns. The consequence of not separating the human subjective and the objective realms is typically one or the other of these alternatives: Either inquiry into nature is restricted to studying the traits that nature shares with humans or it focuses on values in the minds of participants in a certain situation. There is more concern with making sure that the investigators are mentally primed to know what to look for—hierarchy and the rest of those value-laden traits—than with the participants doing a careful investigation in the world of things. If the focus is on the investigator's state of mind, attention shifts away from the actual situation to something else—minds. If model emulation causes a shift away from the objective world, so does this view of knowledge.

What Zhu Xi had called "the investigation of things and exhaustion of principles" and what Wang Yangming called "the extension of knowledge" referred to basic ethical principles that bridge the subjective and the objective, in our analytical parlance. They were rules, standards, and values in the mind and in the world. The content of the Neo-Confucian terms *dao*-mind and "innate moral sense" was prescriptive and also descriptive, with specifications provided mainly for duties.

There is a fact-value fusion in this conception of knowledge. Knowing involves learning through observation a bit about how things actually do behave, and simultaneously understanding both how things should behave according to the standards shared by humans and nature, and how we should behave towards them. Knowledge is not a matter of maximizing one's store of descriptive, empirical facts; collecting examples of perceived relations between events; or compiling records of statistical regularities. Rather, it involves realizing that a plant does go through a seasonal cycle from bulb to sprout to flower to withering, and even more important, recognizing that it *should* do so. The major traits of nature and humans involve both consistent processes (a matter of descriptive fact), *and* ethical purpose, hierarchy, and relational roles (a matter of values). Other traits are trivial. The goal of knowing is not to grasp details about an objective situation. If unpleasant details are uncovered, the goal is to veil them from view. The scope of knowledge shrinks for everyone except sages, who are interested in how nature's patterns all fit together into a purposive whole.

The most important value is a predictable "completion" of process. The ideas of process-to-completeness and consistency provide the content of the technical term *cheng* (integrity) that applies to humans and to nature. The universe possesses consistent processes and patterns as its *shili* (true principles), and *cheng* is one form of the true principles of nature—the others being *ren* (humaneness), and *xing* (having an essential nature). As a value term, *cheng* derives in part from the teleological view of nature, or view of nature as purposive. In this view, all classes of things go through a process to completion akin to the acorn-to-oak process. Things *should* complete their processes and behave in a manner consistent with their kind. Planets and people have roles to fulfill, planets by sticking to their orbits and humans by consistently doing their duties, in the most common example, as father, son, and official.

In studying wild animals, the only important thing is knowing their life cycles, their duties and our duty to them. Their life cycles involve the naturally goal-directed way that the category of things called animals goes about reproducing itself. People should study how to facilitate animals fulfilling their duties of seasonal growth and reproduction without endangerment by hunting at the wrong times. Thus the relevant content of knowledge would include just the basics of their seasonal cycles and the human duty to help them complete their life cycles.

Ordinary people show they are complete by contributing to orderly households and harmonious communities. The elite does so through public service as officials or educators, if they are male. In the modern period societal completeness might be characterized by a rapid increase in production, which would result in the completed state of modernization. Or, it might refer to a way of organizing people that is said to be most progressive. In either case, the value lies with "being complete" and acting consistently. Of course, some models exemplify more specific values as well, such as filiality or loyalty.

The *dao*-mind is the subjective or psychological source for values that perform the controlling function in inquiry. It should control all other psychological activity. Activity, including inquiry into social problems, is significant by being controlled by that *dao*-mind. This means that values drive inquiry, rather than hypotheses as in the scientific method. Values learned from the model or intuited in the *dao*-mind are generally concerned with interpersonal affairs, or matters of hierarchy and role relationships, or processes of biological production and reproduction.

In the context of the Confucian style of inquiry, "to drive inquiry" means that concern with value standards found in those human/heavenly traits should control fact gathering, the determination of cause-effect relations, the prediction of consequences, emotional response to a situation, and analysis. The practical consequence is this: Any facts or actions not relevant to these values are trivialized and likely to be ignored. For example, in studying plants, one may be primarily concerned with their place in providing food as an act of filiality to parents. The value of filiality then determines which aspects of plant life one studies. Or, in evaluating the claims of a young investigator, the nature of his relationship with older investigators may well be the principal concern and the inquiry then reflects little on the object of study.

In the modern period, some of the values have changed, but not the method. Orthodox social values still drive inquiry. Devastating consequences may come of inquiry into societal events when it is driven by values not of science itself—objectivity, free dissemination of information, respect for evidence and for conclusions. Such consequences follow when the driving values are the nonscientific or nonepistemic—process completion, role fulfillment, hierarchy, and the reproduction of life associated with what modern Western philosophers call vitalism. (This is the doctrine that there is more to living organisms than their physiochemical constituents. The perpetuation of their additional vital principle is a cosmic purpose.) Further, as defining features of orthodoxy, the driving social values are not subject to public criticism and evaluation. The negative consequences that often have followed from the Confucian style of inquiry are a result of this fact: When solutions are suggested by inquiry driven by social and political values, there are no permissible alternatives to them.

There is no claim here that modern science or its theses are value-free. The prediction and control of future events are values that scientists employ in choosing between competing hypotheses. Nor are scientists immune from the contextual influences of their own histories, as the occasional inability of those from different schools to agree testifies. On precisely such grounds, Peter Railton reaffirms the currently common position that science is not objective in the popular sense. He argues that the real issue in seeking objectivity has been protecting inquiry from domineering control by something other than the world itself, that is, protecting it from domineering rule by the subjective. We can still adhere to values that permit rather than obstruct self-correcting judgments about objective facts. Hypotheses and reasoning are subjects of public evaluation. Railton prizes the value of "experimentation" with different beliefs and norms.[25] I am also partial to the insight of Jürgen Habermas that certain norms are privileged, namely those that promote communication and the absence of coercion. The choice of hypotheses that arises in investigation is also affected by such values as simplicity and how fruitful a hypothesis is for generating subsequent innovations. These values in operation do not intrinsically distort inquiry. Even if they play a role in our inquiry, the hypotheses that such inquiry generates may still be reliable. That is, they are open to modification as new information comes to light.

My use of the expression "nonscientific values" or "nonepistemic values" in the present context refers to Chinese social roles and other social or political values enforced by official orthodoxy. When nonepistemic values dominate inquiry, they generate hypotheses that do not change as circumstances change. The problem with the Confucian doctrine is its advocacy of the domination of subjectivity and values that may distort our understanding of the way the external world impinges on us. People may continue to look for things that do not exist and point to "signs" of their existence. The Confucian, looking for hierarchy in nature, has long pointed to the fact that heaven is high and earth is low as proof that there is hierarchy beyond the subjective or social world.

Although core values are innate in the *dao*-mind and open to intuition by the learned, models are necessary for ordinary people because their minds are unclear. Imitating the model helps to clarify the mind. This idea is more important in the teachings of Zhu Xi than it is in those of Wang Yangming. At times Wang disdained reliance on models as a substitute for personal intuition, though he also waffled and made a place for both models, texts, *and* intuitionism.[26]

The emotions also were involved in the situation in which subjective factors dominated inquiry. Where the modern Western scientific investigators seek to control their involvement, the Confucian affirmed his legitimate place in the process. He regarded inquiry as a form of empathy with the object being studied. Zhu Xi had used the expression *ticha* (to embody) to depict the mind' s projection into the object, an act of caring for the thing and probing into its natural structure. The fact that Henri Bergson in his twentieth-century writings used a similar idea, translated into Chinese as *tongqing* (sympathy), lent "embodiment" a modern flavor in the eyes of modern Chinese thinkers.

If desirable knowing is empathic (*ticha*), the concern with attaining empathy eliminates from the object of inquiry details or facts about which empathy may be unlikely (the mundane, or the offensive in the eyes of custom). Or, empathy may be incompatible with the detachment that should be part of rigorous scientific inquiry. But it may have positive consequences as well. The treatment of living things that are targets of study may improve if the investigator is empathic.

Likewise, thinking in terms of a unity of man and heaven has its strengths. It forces us to think of the biological interdependency of humans and their physical environment, because there are common interests that bind the two. I believe that it also has its weaknesses and dangers. One danger lies in the idea that there are goals or purposes (processes leading to the completion of goals) in nature. I believe that the attribution of value-laden goals to nature stems from taking a human trait—acting purposively and often *unpredictably*—and attributing it to nature, whose aggregate material particles operate somewhat predictably according to physical laws. (I table such topics as mutations and chaos theory). To look for purpose distracts investigators, leading them to look for things in nature they may never find.

The Confucian epistemology associated with the above style of inquiry is narrow. It poses a limited set of questions about the (assumed) relation between the content of the individual subject' s mind and the structure of the objective world. It asks, "Does the mind accept and act in accordance with such structural traits as purposive consistency, role fulfillment, hierarchy, reciprocal relations, and the nurturance of life?" "Can the mind recognize these in nature or in whatever situation it is investigating?" It guarantees that that structure will be clear to those committed to the right values. It does not favor the questions: "Is there more to the objective world than this?" "Can we continually increase our knowledge of it?" "If so, how?"

In addition, some Confucian thinkers have upheld a hierarchy of knowledge, with technical knowledge at the bottom of the value ladder. Hands-on skills and knowledge derived from inquiry into objective conditions are trivialized, so the scope of knowledge is further narrowed. Typically, a Song Confucian would use the terms deep and shallow to express this difference in worth between forms of knowledge. Deep knowledge develops as we understand how a variety of facts are integrated, rather than by maximizing our detailed acquaintance with any single thing. It is achieved when we understand all of the processes of all of the categories of things and how they are interrelated. Zhu Xi describes this knowledge as the result of the mind passing through (*guantong*) many things like string through holes in coins. The unity of man and heaven suggests the possibility of totalistic knowledge, usually attained only by a few clear-minded sages.

Moreover, some Confucians treated knowledge as equivalent to intention, strange as that may sound to non-Chinese. This is particularly true of Wang Yangming' s school. Wang said that "when a thought is aroused, it is already action," and "[when] only knowledge is mentioned, action is included, and when only action is mentioned, knowledge is included."[27] The implication of his teaching is that the cognitive content and effort of objective study are excluded from the domain of knowledge. Attention is shifted to the subject' s intent and away from the object. Knowledge is seen as a process that occurs during action. Practically, this produced an atypical Confucian distancing from books. Its motto was, in effect, "just do it." In the hands of Wang Yangming, this view of knowledge was a recipe for both impetuous bravery and for confidence that he could succeed in the feat of transforming illiterate minority tribesmen into sages in his place of political exile. Their sagehood would not be based on the verbal knowledge found in books, but on actions geared to improve character.

I will now explain in more detail that Confucian inquiry was not the only style of inquiry in China. The point of doing so is to underscore the fact that there were many levels on which people operated, and their possible assent to the imperial style did not necessarily mean observing it in practice.

Competing Styles of Inquiry

One of the most intriguing alternatives to the imperial style of inquiry was that of the Daoists who both investigated natural phenomena and worked in sophisticated algebraic mathematics. However, I will introduce here a less-studied and possibly more important alternative that was widely practiced by those who gave lip service to the orthodox style. Let me call this alternative the entrepreneurial style of inquiry.

Officials and merchants had an obligation to respect the imperial style but they could also ignore it in practice, proceeding instead with activities that would resolve a problem most efficiently. This does not mean that the imperial style was merely a myth with no operational consequences. As mentioned above, for some officials it was a source of courage and the origin of confidence that, armed with the right ideas, like Wang Yangming, they could prevail against punishment and enemies. Other people, however, acted as though it truly was a myth. For them, people with technical skills, the gathering of facts at the grassroots level, sensitivity to variation, and flexibility in implementing rules were the real keys to success. Let me illustrate how important these mechanisms really were in the economic life of the country.

During much of the nineteenth century, Hankow was central in a national market involving, among other things, trade in wood products, copper and lead, herbs, and tea. The national market employed water transportation, and commercial groups from different areas were linked in cooperative networks. One of the reasons for their success was their access to accurate and timely intelligence about products, markets, transportation, and banking. In the words of William T. Rowe,

> The empire-wide dispersion of such groups was facilitated by rapidly developing networks of commercial intelligence and even more by emergence of a native banking system. Evidence from Hankow thus demonstrates the remarkable responsiveness of Chinese commercial capital to empire-wide market conditions, in an ability to shift investments fluidly from one commodity to another, and indeed from one macroregion to another, as prospects warranted.[28]

Thomas Metzger has described the organizational ability of the Qing dynasty officials charged with shipping salt from the coast of northern Jiangsu province to seven other provinces from 1740–1840.[29] He found that officials lacking skills in commercial affairs turned to merchants who had those skills. Thus there developed a cooperative relation between the two, with powerful merchants acting as middlemen between the state and other shippers. There were some drawbacks to this arrangement in terms of policy coherence, but there was also enough mutual adaptation that the salt was successfully shipped over a vast area. Metzger writes:

> Qing ideology and education precluded the mature combination in one interest group of both political dedication and economically technical skills. Officials were often interested in actively promoting commerce but not in directly engaging in it themselves. Because they therefore often had to recruit persons economically more skillful but politically less dedicated than they, leadership in state commercial organizations tended to lack coherence.[30]

The officials manifested considerable flexibility, adjusting tax rates, for example, to reflect changing economic conditions.[31]

Susan Mann has described how Qing merchants were both demeaned and protected by officials who utilized their knowledge of markets and transportation services.[32] They coped by joining their families with literati elites, so that the boundary line between the classes became obscure. Sometimes they also purchased official titles. At the local level, families with knowledge of local conditions served as officially appointed brokers and solved the problems of regulating markets: management of storage, price monitoring, regulating weights and measures, maintaining roads between markets, and control of outsiders.[33] Participation in guilds or same-name or native-place associations also provided a forum for the exchange of technical information.

The bottom-line motivation for seeking technical knowledge included economic incentives. As Shiba Yoshinobu has pointed out, "By the Song dynasty, the traditional taboo on the overt pursuit of profit had been somewhat relaxed."[34] Those with the rectified minds promoted by the imperial Confucian ideology should not be motivated by profit. But in the real world of operationally oriented officials, those who had to run state enterprises were not deterred from availing themselves of people with technical skills simply because they were merchants. Furthermore, in Qing Statecraft writings, the public interest was a key reason for the positive reevaluation of profit/advantage as a legitimate goal of the Confucian administrator.

Some of the most dramatic examples of inquiry based on comprehensive fact gathering concern water control. Within the Hubei plain, there were vast topographic, social, climatic, and riverine differences from region to region. The problem was always how to protect those differing areas from seasonal floods through a system of dikes. In disrepair because of the dynastic transition, the dikes presented immediate problems to regional irrigation and flood-control efforts. Records from 1395, and from the fifteenth century, track the degree to which officials consulted with locals to gather facts about specific features of the different regions. Acting on the facts they had gathered, the officials successfully completed the construction and repair of a large number of reservoirs, canals, dikes, and embankments. Documents from later years show that officials were required to monitor magistrates on the scene and to keep themselves informed about local conditions, which they forwarded in reports to the capital. When the water control system did not work, it was more often due to political infighting that led to partisan decisions than to a faulty system of inquiry.[35]

In the nineteenth century, the comprador, or Chinese agent for a foreign-owned firm, became a new kind of problem solver. Partially Confucian, he prized filiality, celebrated the birthday of Confucius, and observed the ritual rules of mourning. But he was likely to be an innovative entrepreneur as well. As Yen-p'ing Hao puts it,

> The comprador went one step beyond simple emulation, for each entrepreneur has to consider the nature of the economic problems peculiar to his own enterprise. In other words, an entrepreneur works out new combinations of factors of production and distribution.[36]

If his foreign client needed something, he gathered facts on how to get it; if a new kind business presented itself, such as buying and selling insurance, he figured out how to go about it. The resourcefulness of the

Chinese entrepreneur demonstrated that alternative styles of inquiry could and did coexist with the old Confucian style as China entered the twentieth century.

The persistence of an entrepreneurial culture reinforced this alternative style of inquiry. It required the collection of accurate information and the use of technical skills in banking, transportation and dike repair. However, the Confucian style of inquiry still endured. It was an ideal that could not safely be mocked. For many it was far from being a remote ideal. It certainly inspired leaders of modern China. In the next chapter, we will encounter modern exemplars of the imperial style who operated on several levels at the same time, even using the entrepreneurial style to achieve certain goals.

Evaluation and Outlook

A departure from old premises about knowledge or the move to a new paradigm requires a shift in thinking. Opportunities for change within the Confucian tradition of inquiry include a recognition that the use of models is a mix of blessings and obstructions. In self-cultivation and the socialization of children, models have known efficacy; in problem solving they may be an obstruction to effective inquiry. Another opportunity for departure from old ideas exists in the differentiation of the human and natural, or subjective and objective, realms. An important change would be to overcome the belief in the reality of an objective world with human traits. Not all classical Chinese thinkers blurred the distinction between our minds and the natural world. The Later Mohists affirmed an objective world distinct from our minds.[37] On the cusp of China's early modern period, so did Wang Fuzhi (1619–1693). But the power of the dominant Confucian view over the centuries means that its perspective is the one that has caused much damage and necessitates real change. Contemporary examples of this damage will be explored in chapter 3.

Expectations about the efficacy of mind rectification in the investigation and solution of social problems color the very doctrine of rectification. Without the predictions of wonders the cultivated person can achieve in the solution of social problems, rectification procedures may stand as suitable for goals related to self-cultivation and self mastery. However, given the inflated claims for mind rectification, my criticisms are not inappropriate.[38]

There is a bridge that links the premodern sources of the idea of totalistic structure and the imperial Confucian style of inquiry with the forms of inquiry in the second half of the twentieth century. That bridge lies in the writings of the major political and philosophical figures from the May 4th Movement of 1919 through the 1930s and 1940s. I will now turn to those thinkers who were involved in that transmission. Having crossed that bridge, I will then give examples of how the Confucian approach has affected inquiry into problems prior to, and most significantly, after the death of Mao. I will conclude by identifying two opportunities for change that have begun to emerge.

One is the identification of heaven with objectivity, the human with subjectivity, and a willingness to separate the two. Dividing the subjective and the objective permits people to retain a concern with the interdependency of humans and nature without attributing the same traits to both realms. The objective world can then be understood in its own terms, rather than those of the realm of human social values. The other is the emergence of the value of individual autonomy that now coexists with other values opposed to it. These developments may contribute to the eventual legitimacy of individual autonomy in China, and to acceptance of a process of inquiry that is tolerant of, or even encourages, a variety of theories.

CHAPTER TWO

Modern Exemplars of the Imperial Style

A remarkable list of people helped carry the imperial style of inquiry into and through the twentieth century. Some observers, failing to note this, have attributed its preservation to a minor and uninfluential set of conservative Confucian holdouts. Nothing could be farther from the truth. At the same time, the endurance of the style should not obscure the fact that this was only one approach among many to problem solving. Its chief competition was the scientific methodology being introduced into two types of institutions, universities and medical schools, in the 1920s and 1930s. Nor should its endurance blind us to the fact that one and the same person could well buy into both methodologies, for different purposes.

The significance of universities and medical schools is that they were a kind of intellectual root system to which scientific methodology could be grafted. They made it possible for the scientific approach to be transferred year by year to incoming students and for the records of its implementation to be preserved in the libraries, journals, and memories of the institutions' members. The transformation of universities and hospitals in the 1930s provided the basis for a shift in the pattern of inquiry that began to manifest itself in the 1980s. I will discuss that shift in detail in chapters 4 and 5.

There had been a bias right up to the early 1930s against applied studies. Prior to 1930, not a single Chinese university offered a respectable program in medicine or agriculture, and few students showed much interest in courses in chemistry or biology.[1] However, by the end of the 1930s, two schools had become exemplary centers of science education: National Southeastern University (later renamed National Central University) in Nanking, Jiangsu Province, and Tsinghua University in Peking. At that time, the Ministry of Education of the Nationalist government did a great deal to promote science in these institutions. It shifted resources to schools capable of teaching courses with practical application, especially in agriculture, engineering, and medicine.[2] On the medical front, the Rockefeller Foundation's Peking Union Medical College had begun to flourish in the 1920s. That foundation provided grants that advanced the quality of scientific work in a number of institutions during the period from 1915 to 1933. As Mary Bullock describes it,

> While to the historian much of the research appears procedural, two decades of painstaking, meticulous experiments and uncounted hours of basic research contributed to the impregnation of the scientific method on Chinese soil.[3]

William Henry Welch of Johns Hopkins played a key role in this transfer.

While the hard sciences were embraced in China as a means to modernize its material culture and thereby strengthen the nation, central scientific principles—the separation of desires and values from the objective world, inquiry guided by hypothesis and newly discovered facts rather than by antecedent authority, and the autonomy of the individual investigator—were less prominent in the study of social and political issues. This dual committment to science in material development and to Confucian inquiry in the social arena, both in academic work (for example in psychology and demography) and in political writings, can be seen at various levels from the 1930s onward. Officials, while paying respect to the politically prominent advocates of Confucian inquiry, often went ahead with an approach to problem solving entirely consistent with the style of inquiry found in most Western industrial countries. They relied on a technocratic elite within the government having skills in banking or engineering, for example, to hire a technocratic elite outside the government when their particular skills were needed. The Kuomintang's National Resources Commission wanted to have some kind of state capitalism, but there were no supporting institutions. So in 1936 the Commission entered into a joint Sino-German Three-Year Plan to build steel works, mines, an electrical manufacturing company and the like, in south-central China.[4]

Highest level elites, Chiang Kai-shek (Jiang Jieshi) and his Minister of Education, Chen Lifu, strongly backed such initiatives. But they also perpetuated the imperial Confucian style practices and beliefs in the analysis of objective social and political problems.

Every major Chinese political leader of this century has considered himself to be a philosopher with his own theory of knowledge. Sun Yat-sen, Chiang Kai-shek, and Mao Zedong all wrote about knowledge and had scores of satellite political theoreticians and academic philosophers who amplified their ideas. Their doctrines share remarkable similarities with regard to style of inquiry and have had devastating consequences through their analysis of social problems. These similarities are not surprising, given the common sources in Zhu Xi and especially in Wang Yangming Neo-Confucianism, on which they all drew. The consequences of their approach have been unfortunate, in part because their momentary political power discouraged would-be epistemologists from pursuing divergent approaches. For example, there have been only two notable academic epistemologists who worked along Western philosophical lines during the entire period from 1919 to 1979 (Zhang Dongsun and Jin Yuelin).[5]

In the works of both types of elites, the political and the scholarly, attention shifts from the objective world to the mind and values that drive its inquiry. Often, attention shifts at the outset from the specific objective situation to an individual human model whose mind is to be emulated, or to an authoritative text whose values or situational models are assumedly appropriate guides for dealing with or understanding a particular, immediate problem.

In our century, the three political leaders themselves, Sun Yat-sen, Chiang Kai-shek, and Mao Zedong have been the supreme models. Certain essays of each leader also took on exemplary status, with different selections coming to the fore at different times. Further, each leader identified certain organizations and individuals as worthy of emulation because they embodied the values that the leader wished to communicate. Nongovernmental writers drew their models from a variety of sources. Liang Sou-ming (1893–1988), for example, drew on the "Community Compact," a premodern model of hierarchical, reciprocal obligations and peer pressure for moral reform, as a model for rural social organization. Its most well-known description is in the fifteenth century writings of Wang Yangming. To illustrate the persistence of the imperial style of inquiry in modern times, I will begin by discussing the three political leaders and then turn to other influential thinkers.

Sun Yat-sen

Even the casual student of modern Chinese history is likely to be aware of Sun Yat-sen's debt to Montesquieu (division of power), Henry George (single tax), and to John Stuart Mill (state appropriation of future unearned increases in land value). However, few are aware of the Chinese roots of his doctrines. Had they investigated, they would have found that he also shared the Confucian style of inquiry into problems and their solutions with the other major political leaders of the twentieth century and their associated theoreticians. In spite of his medical education and extensive experience abroad, the premises of the old Confucian style of inquiry emerge clearly in his writings.

In 1918–1919, Sun Yat-sen wrote what is now called *Sun Wen xueshuo* (Writings of Sun Yat-sen) in which he summed up his political epistemology in the phrase, *xing yi zhi nan* (action is easy, knowledge is difficult; hereafter abbreviated as AEKD).[6] "Knowledge" includes, besides scientific principles, an understanding of ideals, goals, and the means to achieve them.[7] This "difficult" knowledge is accessible only to an elite who "know first and are aware first." "Those who do not know can also act" is the title of one chapter in his work on AEKD.[8] So true knowledge is the preserve of the few who make plans and then pass them on to craftsmen. In effect, Sun divided those who know from those who merely act.[9] The former, namely himself and other leaders of his Party, were models in the revolutionary effort.

Sun openly admitted that the intellectual support for this epistemological theory was a political value. In chapter 5 of *Sun Wen xueshuo* he says, "The reason I am not afraid of people being annoyed ... is that I take formulating the theory that 'action is easy and knowledge is difficult' as the necessary road to save China."[10] The political value of saving the country made an epistemological theory acceptable to him, in spite of possible criticisms from others.

The first value that Sun sought to pass from models to people was commitment to AEKD. Others were derived from the kind of holistic structure that had its origins in the commentaries to *The Book of Changes* and was reinforced by Southern Song Confucianism. These values gave content to knowledge. This knowledge included understanding vitalism, the thesis that the production and reproduction of life via a nonphysical force is nature's most important characteristic. This fact links humans and nature. According to Sun, what moves the universe forward is the will to live, not material things such as forces or relations of production, as claimed by Marxists. People's minds should possess the will to live; to be motivated by it was a prized value. His entire doctrine of the "people's livelihood" has this will to live as its basis. In Sun's own words, "Life is the core of the cosmos and the people's life [or livelihood] is the core of society." [11] He also wrote:

> [T]he people's life is central to the advancement of society, society's advancement is central to history, which returns to the fact that the core of history is the people's life, not matter. . . . Past and present, all mankind's effort is for the sake of seeking to exist, and mankind's seeking to exist is the cause of society's advancement.[12]

In other words, there is a metaphysical foundation to one of the Three People's Principles, and it ties Sun into the same perspective as the other leading inheritors of Confucianism in the twentieth century. They share the vitalism and the values associated with it: those of reproduction, nurturance, and preservation of life, as well as the energy involved in accomplishing them. In Sun's case, the value of obedience to knowledgeable leaders is tagged on because they understand how to realize vitalist values. The knowledge that is "difficult" includes, in addition to scientific theory, the metaphysical foundation of these values, and the means to realize them. It is knowledge possessed by the few.

The idea that knowledge is accessible only to an elite not only transforms that elite into models to be emulated by the problem solver. It also carries the conclusion that knowledge is narrow. It does not include skill knowledge, or the skills that make up hands-on technology. Sun treated action (*xing*) of the kind practiced in applied theory as mechanical, often akin to the instinctive behavior of animals. It is guided by "knowledge" that is superficial, not penetrating the essence of its subject matter.[13] However, as Hu Shi noted in criticizing Sun's doctrine, if "[theoretical] knowledge is difficult, then its application (as action) may be equally difficult," as any clinical specialist or thoracic surgeon can testify. The theory that Sun counted as knowledge was separate from action, and so he did not appreciate how action can be difficult.[14] To strip applied skills from knowledge is to emasculate scientific investigation and application. It equally denigrates the clinician's laboratory work and the sociologist as participant observer.

It is not enough, then, for a modern theory of knowledge to praise science, as Sun surely did, and say that all true knowledge comes from science. It is not enough, first, because in Sun's doctrine, the view of knowledge that should guide the social scientist is derived not from science but from a political value. In other words, it serves values other than that of objectivity. Ironically, Sun Yat-sen, the medically trained statesman, did not comprehend the place of technical skill in the advancement of knowledge.

Inheriting the Confucian style of inquiry, Sun attributes success to the mind's being armed with the values I have mentioned. Failure results when it is not so armed. In a remarkable analysis of the failure of attempts to "establish the country" after the success of the 1911 revolution, Sun Yat-sen explained the cause as "mistakes of thought and a slack will."[15] He said that "the basis for establishing the country must emanate from the mind."

This focus on the mind as an explanation ignores these objective considerations: the impact of humiliation by foreign powers since the

Opium Wars on China's elites, which in turn weakened their stature among the populace; the inadequacy of traditionally educated gentry as leaders in the rural areas from which they came and in the cities; warlords or regional authorities and their power over provincial finances; inexperience with legal codes; changing economic conditions due to foreign imports; and finally, political factions. Thus Sun's style of inquiry perpetuates the obstructions to objective social analysis begun in the first place by the premodern obsession with what is in the minds of participants in an event under consideration. In this way it ignores precisely those variables that would contribute to the Communist success and the Nationalist failure in the 1940s.

Sun went on to say that "a human is a vessel of the mind" and "the mind is the source of all things"—hence, it should have been the source of practical success in establishing the country. This confers special worth on the human mind and also raises the concrete question: What was in the mind that caused the failure? Sun's answer was twofold: there was intellectual misunderstanding about the fact that "knowledge is difficult [leave it to the elite] but action is easy [so just act]," and this principle did not command widespread approval. Sun held that the guarantee for success in establishing the country was a correct comprehension of AEKD. From this understanding, the people "will not fear anything and will take pleasure in action." [16]

Chiang Kai-shek

Like most of us, Chiang Kai-shek probably had mixed motives. He perpetuated Confucian inquiry with its glorification of rectifying minds because it had political utility. It helped to legitimize him as something more than just another warlord. Instead, he could characterize himself as one in a long line of "Confucian generals" (see below). At the same time, he may well have been committed to those teachings. There is no way to substantiate the claim that his Confucianism was all theater. He gave every evidence of treating its rituals seriously.

Chiang systematically linked the topics of models to the topic of learning to control the mind (*zhixin*), thereby laying out the technique for this practice. In lectures and writings from the late 1930s he begins with the argument that in order to defeat Japan, the first task of the Chinese is to improve their morality: "Why are we Chinese oppressed by the Japanese? It is because the Chinese people do not discuss morality! The indigenous morality of the past has been lost." [17] He goes on to encourage his followers to read books by two people. One is by Sun Yat-sen, and the other is by himself, about his own choice of models: *Zengbu Zeng Hu zhibing yulu (Additions to "Quotations Concerning the Way to Control Troops, by Generals Zeng Guofan and Hu Linyi")*. Zeng Guofan and Hu Linyi are known as the mid-nineteenth century's "Confucian Generals" (*rujiang*), a stature Wang Yangming had achieved several centuries earlier. These Confucian Generals stood for traditional Confucian society and its values. They were the principal models from which officers could learn to rectify their minds and commit their troops to realizing the values for which Sun stood. Chiang wrote,

> In controlling the army we first must control the minds, and if you want to control the troops you must definitely first control your own mind, and then carry out your policy. If your own mind is not good and you cannot rectify it, then those under your command whom you teach will not be any good and cannot succeed at anything. Control of the mind, then, is the most important basis of success for soldiers.[18]

So leaders should be living models for the people. The values to be communicated include, in addition to those already discussed, "being a true person" and following the Three Peoples Principles of Sun Yat-sen.

The textual source that Chiang treated as providing the foremost theoretical model is *The Great Learning*, one of the earliest texts to make the linkage between a rectified mind and practical success at home or in governing. Note his connection of this text to science and to "actual discoveries":

> But you must realize that the meaning and knowledge contained in what the current age calls by the name "science" was not discovered by foreigners. Our Chinese ancients emphasized it thousands of years ago. Not only were there great actual discoveries but also there were theoretical revelations. Among them, the most basic and most important was a book, i.e. *The Great Learning*. I often say that *The Great Learning* should be called *The Scientific Great Learning*.... We can say that *The Great Learning* is basic scientific theory.[19]

Through his focus on models and mind rectification, Chiang explicitly diverts his audience's attention from the objective situation to what is in their minds,

> No matter what the situation or demand for knowledge, you must always first begin the effort of your search with the thing close at hand [the mind]. ... If we ignore this and pay no attention to it and instead focus on the external thing that is very profound and difficult ... there definitely will not be a good result.[20]

> The source of knowledge lies in the original nature [the original pure mind] of mankind and does not need to be sought outside of it. On the surface, when we seek knowledge we must accept the experience and lessons of other people and study foreign science and techniques. But in reality, if knowledge is not 'self-derived' [i.e., innate and intuitive] it is not true knowledge. Only 'self-derived' knowledge is true knowledge, and it is not just true knowledge but it is also easy to practice.[21]

As for defining the scope of knowledge, where Sun's political epistemology centered on AEKD, Chiang Kai-shek accepted that principle but reduced it to a simpler one: *lixing* (practice), redefining in the process action and knowledge.[22] In so doing, he reduced the scope of knowledge even beyond that of Sun's already truncated theory, making it considerably narrower than is common in modern Western science. There are two traditional claims that undlie his theory.

First, Chiang held that knowledge is only concerned with *xing* or *lixing* (practice—action or behavior), and he redefined *xing* so that it conforms to the fact-value fusion.[23] Only acts involving integrity and humaneness are worthy of the name practice or action. The values that identify practice are the cosmic ones: *cheng* (integrity, completeness, consistency) and *ren* (humaneness, meaning the full development and protection of "natural" life processes or those that accord with natural structures). So a vitalistic focus on life and the teleological focus on advancement to goals are part of the picture.

Second, drawing on the traditional assumption that there is a unity of heaven and man, Chiang also asserted that acts with integrity and humaneness participate in the work of heaven.[24] In this scheme, leaders claim to know the trajectory for individuals and societies and also the kinds of actions that advance the life process to completion. They know the scope of *xing* (practice). Thus, only social acts covered by official rules of conduct constitute practice. Such acts are part of natural life and simultaneously are a means to improve it. Other behaviors are neutral and are termed *dong* (movement). Practice purposively promotes those acts that fulfill natural goals, thereby improving human life. Specifically, this meant implementing Chiang's policies to fight the Japanese and to establish the Three People's Principles, because those policies promoted the life process for the Chinese people.[25]

If knowledge was about *xing*, behavior that did not manifest its values (*cheng, ren*) was trivialized.[26] It was mere *dong*, not an object of knowledge, and it was to be ignored or repressed. *Xing* is moral action, and because morality has to do with human life in many dimensions, the acts and facts of interest in scientific inquiry may be of only secondary interest to those wishing to know about proper practice.

Not only did Chiang go beyond Sun in chopping "knowledge" out of the AEKD slogan, he also redefined knowledge as equivalent to intention, stripping it of cognitive substance. He wrote that practice includes knowing, intention, and will.[27] To have an intention is the same as to have the knowledge provided by the innate moral sense. In this way, right intention can replace exhaustive inquiry for those seeking knowledge. In Chiang's own words, "practice is the same as intention [*xinyi*]" and "to have the intention is to have innate moral knowledge [*liangzhi*]."[28] Equating knowledge with the intention to act derives from premodern Confucian attempts at an alternative to the Buddhist view of knowledge as silent insight. It encourages active social participation, but not objective analysis or inquiry.

Because intention emerges easily as action, the Marxist theoretician, Ai Siqi, says that Chiang reduces Sun's AEKD to "action is easy."[29] Cultivate good intentions and both knowledge and action are assured. In the end there is no encouragement here of rigorous objective study, especially on matters of interest to the social scientist.

Chiang Kai-shek's statement of faith in the power of mind or spirit over matter could have passed for one by Mao or Mao's one-time chosen successor, Lin Biao, after 1958. Chiang held that, "Using the magic of spiritual strategy, we can cause China, which is not equal to the enemy in weapons, economy, or industry, to have a final victory [over the enemy, i.e., the Japanese]."[30] There are several ways of describing the content of that spirit.

To call it *cheng* (integrity, completeness, consistency) is a point Chiang shares with his Minister of Education, Chen Lifu. Adding to its original meaning, they said that *cheng* involves the *power* of nature working through the individual, which can conquer anything. Thus, to earlier meanings is added the energy or power found in nature when nature is not lacking any of its parts. Humans might tap this energy. It could overcome Japan and successfully secure the country.

This value of integrity feeds directly Chiang's style of problem solving. Integrity is the source of the energy that enables a rectified mind to proceed to the realization of goals. Broadly, it is the motive or energy that enables a person to go through the stages of life and also an awareness of the motive and commitment to complete that process. A person with integrity is able to help heaven in the completion of its processes. In turn, the cosmic significance of one's own acts as an individual are expanded when they are motivated by integrity. They become part of the cosmic processes, especially those concerned with life and reproduction. Further, integrity is a cosmic trait that introduces order into chaos, energizing all things to move into predictable classes with their predictable processes to completion. To possess integrity is to be able to change the world. Such was the claim of Chiang Kai-shek and his Minister of Education.

A second magical property of mind derives from entertaining the correct meaning of action or practice as in AEKD. Chiang stated that the failures of the Kuomintang (KMT) could be traced to bad ideas, namely that the KMT comrades lost their momentum because they did not understand the meaning of practice.[31] Its meaning may be variously phrased as "that which accords with heavenly nature," "the goal of all movement," or "actions that manifest the energy to survive, reproduce, and develop all of life's possibilities".

A third source of mental power, said Chiang, is a knowledge of Chinese philosophy. "Our greatest danger is that educators and intellectuals do not sufficiently study [Chinese] philosophy."[32] Given the fact-value fusion, "understanding" means awareness of and approval of relevant Chinese philosophical positions on the style of inquiry into problems and their solutions. With it, he said, we Chinese can establish a nation and the revolution can succeed. He continued with an observation that foreshadowed the "red and expert" discussions of later decades: "biologists, physicists, and mechanical engineers should master the fundamentals of their learning [Chinese philosophy]; then their teaching and learning can have real results."[33] Of course, the central idea in Chinese philosophy to which he referred is mind control or rectifying the mind.

Like the doctrines of any central political figure, the epistemological views of Sun Yat-sen and Chiang Kai-shek were amplified by a host of other significant and influential thinkers. Politicians and scholars made a common cause of undercutting objectivity. In the scholars' hands as well as in those of the politicians, to varying degrees, the key feature of inquiry is not objectivity but letting nonscientific values shape the search for facts. It is not generally known that the chief non-Marxist philosophical spokesmen for the fact-value fusion within the Confucian tradition (Xiong Shili and He Lin) continued to write and publish in this vein even after the establishment of the People's Republic of China. Among the philosophical associates of the political leadership, some stood on their own as independent thinkers and respected scholars. Others were political theoreticians in government education or propaganda work. Thus, the epistemologies of Sun Yat-sen and Chiang Kai-shek are to be found in fleshed-out and developed form outside, as well as inside, the political sphere. However, there is considerable overlap between the independent thinkers and the propagandists.

For example, it might be tempting to brush off the widely promoted philosophical positions of Chen Lifu on the grounds that he was a bureaucrat, not a scholar. However, in some of their content they are remarkably similar to the ideas of Xiong Shili, one of twentieth century China's most respected philosophers. This is not surprising, given that one of Xiong's star pupils, Tang Junyi, reportedly helped Chen with his writings. In his memoir, Chen recalls,

> While Minister of Education, in the Ministry I found a young man named T'ang Chün-i who was an editor and versed in philosophy. I invited him home, and for half an hour each day I talked and he took notes. . . .[34]

Both Chen and Xiong drew from the same sources, which shows the power of these sources (*Doctrine of the Mean, The Book of Changes*, Consciousness Only Buddhism, Song-Ming ideas of the innate moral sense, and European vitalism). I want first to touch on both Xiong and Chen as a way of showing that ideas central to the old style of inquiry were valued both by one of modern China's most respected philosophers (teacher not only of Tang, but also of Mou Zongsan, another of China's influential post World War II philosophers), and by one of its most bureaucratically influential officials. They not only shared a holistic worldview characterized by vitalism and teleology, they also agreed that there are two linked keys to practical success. One of these is the cultivation of *cheng* in the mind, thereby enabling one to draw on cosmic energy. The other is ensuring that the moral mind is in control of inquiry. In short, Xiong and Chen shared an investment in totalism and the Confucianism that it supports. I will now take a more detailed look at their positions, beginning with Xiong.

Xiong Shili

Until his death in 1968, Xiong was able to continue writing on and publishing his decidedly non-Marxist doctrines. The reason is not simply that his treatment of inquiry and knowledge share so much with other prominent political and academic figures; it is also because he lived in China, where patronage counts, and he had powerful patrons. Dong Biwu—who passed the first-degree in the imperial examinations, was a founder of the Chinese Communist Party in Shanghai in 1921, and from 1956 until his death was a member of the Politburo and Vice President of China—was a friend from the 1911 Hubei anti-Manchu revolution.[35] Guo Mojo and Chen Yi, Vice Premier and Foreign Minister, were friends.

Xiong's favorite textual model was the teleological and vitalist structure of the universe presented in *The Book of Changes*. While he rejected Western teleological theories, he accepted the principle that the universe exists for the purpose of the production and reproduction of life. This informed any inquiry that could be made into the empirical world. He also insisted that there is a relevant and preexisting framework, model, or ideal that can be applied to any situation being studied. For example, in talking about reading he says,

> Everyone who reads a book must rely on his subjectivity [ideas from his own mind] and the objective aspect of inquiry. I will first speak about the subjective. The reader's mind needs to have an already prepared model [*mofan*], just as in building a house, there must be a fixed basis [design] before the ridgepole and beams are set up. This is called the model. . . . Without a model, without a plan, one is just mindlessly reading books, whether by ancients or moderns. A person on reading a book may blindly absorb the meaning of that one book. If he reads two books, he seems blindly to absorb the meaning of those two books. This can be called being a book bug [flitting from one book to the next].[36]

Xiong applies this approach to his own ethnographic analysis of China. His model is a unified China. Starting with this value-laden model, he selects facts to show that all of the races in China (Han, Manchu, Mongol, Tibetan and Hui) have the same ethnic origin, so they form one family or one bloodline. Although several times admitting that this is his own hypothesis for which he does not have complete evidence, he asserts that the value of unity in contemporary China requires that the hypothesis be viewed as confirmed.[37]

This approach flows easily into a belief in the power of minds armed with the right values. He notes that "whoever writes a history must possess the basic spirit that saturates all events and the figures in it." Today, he says, that spirit is loyalty to the country and the people. Such spirit in a historical work can "release the power of the people," thereby saving China from foreign enemies.[38]

There was also faith that by paying attention to the cultivation of the values of *cheng* and *gong* (impartiality) in the mind, the Chinese people could protect and firmly establish their nation. One cultivates *cheng* by uncovering the "original mind" (original substance) that is in everyone. In seeking to cultivate integrity, the individual could consult Wang Yangming and Zeng Guofan as vital models. They in turn learned about the "original mind" from the early Confucian models such as Mencius.[39]

Xiong's cosmology encourages participatory engagement in life because he unifies and refuses to separate the source of order and the operation of orderly change. (Xiong's source of order is *ti*, commonly translated as "substance"; he also refers to it as "original substance" or "original mind." Orderly change, *yong*, is usually rendered as "function"). The source of order moves. So the world of change is the only world. There is no need to "return to the origin" conceived as some other realm or "return to quietude" as the Buddhists sought to do.

Xiong consistently argues that his philosophy of a unified totality promotes science because it is not a transcendentalism.[40] Furthermore, he says it eschews subjectivity because it encourages the individual to cause his mind to merge with or sympathetically penetrate external things. He advocates "the objective method," to which the "original mind" contributes hypotheses about objective things.[41]

But like all the other modern Confucians, he fails to see that avoiding transcendentalism and encouraging participatory engagement in the world do not solve the problem of how to know objective situations. Rather, the problem lies with his flawed epistemology and style of inquiry. It lies with a doctrine of a moral mind that controls and thereby delimits objective inquiry, and with a penchant for defining "pure truth" and "things" in terms of human relations, thereby severing inquiry from the rest of the world that is not obviously involved in such relations.

His "New Idealist" cosmological structure in fact changes none of the fundamentals about the human mind that have existed all along in imperial Confucianism. The ruler-ruled metaphor for the mind inherited from Zhu Xi and others endures, as vital as ever.[42] And the results are the same: The scope of an investigator's inquiry will be limited to the social role realm of concern, to the innate moral sense, the ruler that resides in the "original mind" and controls all other psychological activity, including inquiry. The content of this innate sense includes the standard Neo-Confucian list of values: humaneness, courage, and filial love as the starting point of ethics, social hierarchy, the goodness of human nature, altruism, interdependence, sincerity, selflessness, and the nurturing of life.[43]

The "original mind" as *zhu* (ruler), possesses *zhi* (wisdom). When we inquire into the objective world, we gain *zhishi* (knowledge) which is a reflection of that world. Ordinary knowledge as distinct from wisdom is the result of *xixin* (the habitual mind) responding mechanically to external things. This mind can cause good or evil, and it must be kept under the control of the ruling mind. Only the ruling mind can integrate individualized data about things gained by the habitual mind and illuminate the principles in things, thereby forming wisdom. Only the ruling mind can "merge with things" and illuminate the principles in them.[44]

This wisdom that controls knowledge is moral understanding: "It is evident that wisdom and morality [*daode*] basically are one thing. They cannot be divided into two."[45] So the acquisition of objective knowledge should be guided by moral principles that determine its range of inquiry and its application. Westerners routinely say the application of technical knowledge helps to increase that knowledge or adds to it. People learn by doing. However, as Xiong would have it, technical knowledge should be controlled by nonscientific moral principles that may limit the mode of application and what we learn from it.

Citing the authority of Wang Yangming, Xiong wrote, "When *liang-zhi* (the innate moral sense) is ruling, then all knowledge is the functioning of the moral sense."[46] He illustrates with an example of a lawyer and a physician who may use their technical knowledge without the control of the moral sense.[47] The message is, never allow knowledge of the objective world and the controlling moral truths to be separated. Ensuring control by the moral sense is the dominant concern. Other than traditional remarks about having sympathy for the object of one's investigation, the methodology of inquiry is ignored.

Once again, then, in Xiong's case we find an influential thinker advocating that nonscientific values—those in the moral mind—should drive inquiry into the facts of a situation. The consequence of such inquiry is to narrow the scope of knowledge. Those consciously held values derive from models or ideals passed on in the Confucian school.

Xiong's style of inquiry derives from his view of models, his clinging to belief in a ruling "original mind" that can be the source of energy—and hence of human motivation—and from the values that he believes should drive inquiry. If the "original mind" is in part the energy that Confucian vitalists routinely attribute to the structure of the universe, it is individuated in a person's mind as both moral intuitions and as motivation. It is informed motivation or zeal. This means that a person can be energized and retain faith by virtue of the knowledge that this zeal comes from something bigger than his individual self. Being in touch with the energy that accounts for the appearance of life, the individual will necessarily promote the welfare of all, nurturing life.

Needless to say, the hierarchy of types of truth that generates a narrow view of knowledge also pervades Xiong's work. He says that what Westerners seek through science is a so-called "truth" and "the meaning of this so-called truth basically is devoid of good and bad."[48] Chinese, in contrast, seek philosophical truth. He notes, "This truth is absolute and pure. From the beginning its nature is always pure. Therefore it is also good. The Confucians may also call it *cheng*. This means a manifestation of both truth and goodness."[49] Another limitation on the scope of inquiry into truths is then revealed when Xiong says that "philosophical truth is always practiced in daily human interactions through human relationships."[50] This supports the priority of studying topics involving human relationships, possibly to the exclusion of the nonhuman variables that affect humans.

Xiong's limited view of objective inquiry renders him oblivious to all the possible obstructions to a person pursuing his own welfare concerns. Among these is the lack of a detailed and comprehensive empirical grasp of the specific problems he will face.

Chen Lifu

Chen Lifu, trained as a mining engineer, served as Chiang Kai-shek's Minister of Education from 1938–44, and continued thereafter to supervise educational affairs. The influence of *Doctrine of the Mean* and *The Book of Changes*, the two authoritative texts on which Xiong relied, are also evident in Chen's writings.

The universe was understood to be in a constant state of change, explained in terms of the inseparable categories of the source of order and operations of orderly change (substance and function). Like Xiong, Chen used the Buddhist analogy of the ocean and its waves to illustrate the relation between the one and the many changing things; all are integrated as a whole. More often than Xiong, he applied the term *cheng* to "original substance," but it remained the source of order in change.[51] Also like Xiong, Chen's philosophy was vitalistic in that life is an attribute of "original substance."[52] The cosmos is teleological.[53] Man's nature is linked to the cosmos, so man shares in that teleology; his job is to assist with the processes of life. This cosmology supports the traditional role-based ethics to which Chiang looked for social discipline and stability. The relationships of father-son, older and younger brothers, and husband-wife, stabilize the continually changing cosmological stream of life.[54]

Like many writers, Chen beat the drum for Chiang's policies, reasoning that the way to assist in heaven's reproduction process or in nurturing life was to act (*xing*), where "practice" or "action" meant to carry out Sun Yat-sen's policy of the "people's livelihood."[55] In his official position Chen lectured to the Central College of Politics (*Zhongyang zhengzhi xuexiao*). Those lectures were turned into a major treatise, *Vitalism* (*Weishenglun*), which contains all of the above ideas. In a 1938 proposal for education at various levels, Chen flagged *cheng* as central to the curriculum. He also wrote that the aim of education in China was to help illuminate the *innate* integrity in the human mind.[56] That innate light in the mind is the ever-burning descendant of the ruling *dao*-mind made famous by Zhu Xi. Chen seemed to say that the aim of education is to enable people to clear the mind and to let it rule.

Chen used his holistic cosmology to support Chiang Kai-shek's style of inquiry into problems. He thereby bolstered a sense of discipline, courage, and commitment to the policies of Chiang Kai-shek in the face of the Japanese and the Communist threats. He argued that if the Chinese people understood the true meaning of the motive force (*cheng*) that stems from "original substance" and bear it in mind, their renaissance would necessarily follow.[57] In humans this force manifests itself as, among other things, self-discipline. Chen promoted *The Great Learning*'s faith in a progression from rectified minds to political success.

He Lin

He Lin (1902–1993) was another central figure in promoting ideas about knowledge similar to those of Sun Yat-sen and Chiang Kai-shek. His name is little known in the West, but he was a highly respected translator of Hegel and Spinoza, honored by Chiang Kai-shek and consulted by Mao after 1949. He provided the sophisticated philosophical basis for AEKD and for Chiang's reformulation of it.[58] He was able to use his commentaries on the Western works as a vehicle for conveying his own ideas. So important was he as a bridge to Western philosophy, that almost every Chinese interested in Western philosophy in general, in German works in particular, and in their Western interpreters (e.g., C. I. Lewis) used He Lin's books. This included ordinary students and the supreme political leaders. He was not a bureaucrat (like Chen Lifu) but a distinguished, independent thinker who arrived at positions that converged with those of Sun and Chiang rather than followed them. This fact suggests that, regarding modern Chinese inquiry, the Confucian heritage is not merely a tool of isolated political leaders. It has been and continues to be widely and deeply shared across the professional spectrum. This helps to explain the breadth and depth of the obstacle it poses to the objective study of social problems.

He Lin subscribed to the principle that humans need models in order to cultivate their minds. The basic theory runs, "because every single thing has its own standard, its own model [*mofan*], if we want to deal well with a thing, we must take [grasping] its model as our goal."[59] According to He Lin, Zeng Guofan took the philosophy of Song Confucians such as Cheng Yi and Zhu Xi as his model. Prior to 1949, He Lin also advocated taking Sun Yat-sen and Chiang Kai-shek as the models of persons who are best at applying the intuitional doctrines of Lu Xiangshan

(1139–1193) and Wang Yangming. He also said that Chiang best understood the exemplary status of *The Great Learning*. Overall, He Lin's models are the patriarchs of philosophical schools: the Ru (Confucians) of the Zhou period, Lu and Wang as proponents of mind control and innate moral knowledge, and Sun and Chiang as their modern descendants. Thus, models were fit into a patriarchal lineage created from the Confucian doctrinal legacy.[60] He's lineage suggests that he saw Confucian orthodoxy reformulated in the "new orthodoxy" of Sun's Three People's Principles.[61] In another essay, we learn from him how models should influence our inquiry into the facts of a situation:

> *The reflection of ideals [lixiang or models, namely, the Three People's Principles] in facts.* In order to understand facts thoroughly, there must be an ideal form [to our inquiry]. There must first be the ideal for understanding and controlling nature, and then there appear the facts; we must first have the ideal [model] for reforming society, and afterwards we can pay attention to the investigation and the reform of social facts. The truer our ideal [note the fact-value fusion], the more precise our grasp of the facts. The ideal can [help us to] determine the rules and the forms for understanding facts, so that all those we collect will correspond to the form of the ideal and be integrated into systematic knowledge. Not only does the ideal not run counter to facts, indeed, it can help us grasp and control them.[62]

In line with old concepts about investigating and solving problems, these model figures and their ideals provide the content of the "spirit" on which any material success in modernizing China would have to be based.

> The new Chinese philosophy advocates that everything must be established on a basis of rationality and on the basis of spirit. Without spirit, there will be nothing. And only with a spiritual basis is there a solid basis. Revolution involves revolutionizing the mind . . . Therefore, our new philosophy is definitely not opposed to material construction, rather it seeks a material construction founded on a spiritual basis. In reality, unless we have spirit, we cannot explore and control the material world. In order to industrialize China, and with effort, to investigate science, we must make an effort in spirituality.[63]

That spiritual basis was the Three People's Principles of Sun Yat-sen.

He Lin's system is also known as New Idealism. It centers on what the mind contributes to our interpretation of the world. To the foundation provided by Zhu Xi and, especially, Wang Yangming, it adds new elements from Kant and Hegel. He Lin claims that the Chinese contribute the mind's a priori acquaintance with moral principles, while the Germans focus on the mind's role in seeing scientific structure in the world, including space and time.[64] He Lin's motive was to return Chinese philosophy to the correct road, namely, the Wang Yangming road, and to broaden and modernize it.[65] The institutional vehicle for his mission was the Society for the Translation of Western Philosophy, founded in 1941 (in 1949 merged with Peking University's Liberal Arts Graduate School). Demonstrative of his impact is the fact that in the most comprehensive collection of articles on philosophical topics between 1919–1949, one whole volume is devoted to He Lin.[66]

With their foundation in Wang Yangming-type assumptions about the innate moral mind and German ideas that were so congenial to them, He's teachings became yet another obstacle to the empirical study of social problems. We discover this when we look at his claims about knowledge.

The knower must focus not only on facts but also on values. These values are not necessarily those of science. This is evident in the terminology he uses. Zhu Xi's *tianli* (heavenly principles) becomes *yuzhou yizhi* (the cosmic will), which is embedded in humans as *liangxin* (their "good minds").[67] Teleology saturates his system, so the familiar value, completion of process, orients the investigator's studies of any natural changes. The investigator must remain mindful of the completed forms of different categories of things and keep track of whether or not what he studies is completing its process. Indeed, the kind of knowledge in which a reasoning person should be interested is theoretical knowledge, not practical reason. And this theoretical knowledge includes the ideal forms that classes of things should take. The fact-value fusion is apparent in the following passage:

> The nature of a thing [*xing*] represents why a thing is the way it is [a factual matter] and also the essential factor according to which it should be as it is [a value matter]. The nature is the original principle or model that arranges all changes and development of a thing. All things, no matter how they act or develop, in the end cannot escape from the scope of their nature. But the nature, on the one hand, is the essential substance that a thing already has while, on the other hand, it is the ideal [*lixiang*, a value term] or model [*fanxing*, valueless, the pattern according to which it is as it is] that a thing must realize.[68]

There is a clear echo here of Zhu Xi's theory that all things embody the principle (*li*) of their type, a principle that fuses facts and values. One discovers the "natures" of things in large part through attention to the mind rather than through objective study. The value of completion is called realizing the "nature." In the case of humans, that fulfillment includes performing role duties, having an aesthetically pleasing cosmic perspective, and acting rationally. Any study of a social problem must relate the facts studied to these values.[69]

There is a place for objective study in the methodology advocated by this intuitionist, and it has some merits. He Lin regarded intuition as a way of using "rational sympathy" to investigate things. He was inspired by Zhu Xi's idea of investigating by *ticha* (projecting the self into things) and by Bergson's idea of sympathy. Understanding objective things must be based on love and sympathy for them. Underlying this method is the assumption of heaven-man totalism, because such sympathy involves understanding how things fit together as a whole.[70] A valid point may exist here, that feeling for an object positively affects cognition. But this point is not developed.

Still, the primacy of understanding innate features of the mind deflects the investigator's attention from his object. His aim is not simply to do careful objective study but to use objective study as a means for improving introspective knowledge of the mind. Using Hegelian language, He Lin says that the objective world expresses the subjective. Natural things manifest subjective aesthetic values. Created things embody the individual's spirit. We continually project our values on the world.[71]

Unlike Hegel, for whom the spirit manifest in the objective world is God, He Lin held that spirit in the world is man's logical mind. As the mind conceives, so goes the world. And that mind's categories or concepts "rule" the objective world—a metaphor derived from Zhu Xi's idea of *dao*-mind or ruler. He meant that it organizes knowledge and evaluates. The mind and things stand in a ruler-ruled, or source and its operations, relation. "The mind is the essential part of things and things are the manifestation of the mind."[72] Therefore, the mind has primary worth. Knowing the mental categories is critical since, being simultaneously moral and scientific, they are the a priori conditions for the rules of morality and laws of nature.[73] Any objective study leads necessarily back to the ruling mind, to "subjectivity." When we look for the content of this moral knowledge we find that it is embodied in *li*[a] (rules of propriety, which are eternal principles), or *li*[b] (patterns that change in historical time), and social role duties and virtues. An objective situation that accords with *li*[b] is a good situation. There is justification here for intellectuals, the specialists on the mind, leading other people.

The human mind, cleared of material desires, having an innate structure of models or ideals ruling its search for facts, can accomplish wonders. It can know the laws of nature and of human society, through introspection.[74] Following them, it will be successful, though He Lin's students learned no way of interacting with the objective world in seeking those laws. Having first taken this position in 1932, he still held to it in a 1984 article on the patriotism of the German thinker Fichte in Germany's struggles with France:

> He [Hegel] is similar to Fichte, holding that when one's material power is not as good as the enemy's, one should strive to conquer the opponent through spiritual and moral power. When in actual and political life spiritual power is given its proper play and function, we may gradually catch up with and even surpass the enemy in 'external tools,' in material conditions. This idea contains some reasonable elements for a situation in which the enemy is strong and we are weak.[75]

In a different context, a commentator wrote that He Lin had tried to get people to view the mind as ruler, organizer, and judge because he wanted people "to feel the importance of spirit in order to strengthen its power to conquer nature, and to strengthen confidence in reviving national culture."[76] If people's ideas are correct, correct social and political actions and institutions will inevitably follow.[77] To conclude, there are clearly differences between the styles of inquiry of He Lin on the one hand, and Chiang on the other. He Lin gave primacy to knowing; Chiang cared more about action. What they share is a belief in a priori principles that impose a nonempirical order on the objective world. They share a belief that facts and nonscientific values coexist and the person investigating objective social problems must search for both. Those nonscientific values may prevent facts from being ordered according to their own logic. Facts irrelevant to those nonscientific values may be ignored. He and Chiang also shared a belief in the primacy of "subjectivity," in the sense that a morally upright mind can overcome any objective situation.

Liang Shuming

Liang Shuming (1893–1988) has been called "the last Confucian." However, this designation may have been awarded prematurely, since Confucianism has flourished since his death, and most likely will continue to flourish long after mine. Liang came from the family of a court official. In 1917 he became professor of Buddhism at Peking University. His commitment to Confucianism, however, was unshakable, especially after the suicide of his Confucian father. In the 1930s he believed that the Chinese countryside would be the center for revived Confucian values if the peasants received proper teaching and were better organized. He set himself the task of initiating such a program. Accordingly, he established the Rural Reconstruction Research Institute in Shandong Province.

Liang took as his cosmology the vitalism of Zhu Xi and Wang Yangming, tempered with a dash of Henri Bergson. One of his textual authorities, predictably, was *The Book of Changes*. The organizational model that inspired the values he sought to impose in Shandong was the *xiangyue* (community compact), about which both Zhu and Wang had written and Wang had acted on. Important studies of Liang and of this model have been written by Western scholars.[78] Led by paternalistic elders, the community compact took the moral transformation of its members as its goal and mutual instruction or criticism as its means.

This model has the appearance in social form of the structure that Liang attributed to the mind, namely, the instruction of inferiors by an enlightened guide. In the mind, two faculties stand in a hierarchical relation to each other. *Lizhi* (the intellect) is something like what Westerners would call practical rationality. It involves knowledge about how to do something, knowledge of the utility or consequences of acts or decisions, and it includes analysis. Intellect has been cultivated by Westerners, according to Liang, and accounts for their material success. However, he maintained that it stands subordinate to *zhijue* or *lixing* (intuition). Intuition is something like impartial moral judgment. It also includes the ability to have a feel for the cosmic pulse of life, so there is an emotional component to it.[79]

The significant thing for our purposes is that the status and content of intuition generate the same consequence I have noted for all the examples above: a limitation of the scope of inquiry. Intuition should give orders to the intellect, doing what I have called driving inquiry. Intuition is concerned only with interpersonal affairs. The result is that priority in knowing goes only to facts relevant to human moral issues.

The community compact model provided Liang with the organization through which the dominance of intuition over the mere study of cause-effect relations could be institutionalized. Simultaneously, that model introduced a critical ingredient in the old Confucian ideas about inquiry. This is the confidence that when the minds of people have the right motives and beliefs (taught in the community under the leadership of the elders as patriarchal instructors), solutions to practical problems in the objective world will necessarily follow. The community compacts provided a forum for raising the "energized will" (*qizhi*) of the people.[80] As Liang put it,

> How do we let the people live fully? We must arouse the spirit of the Chinese people; how do we arouse that spirit? We must try to draw on the power in people's lives and elevate their energized will. . . . [Therefore the

> problem of the economy] ultimately is a problem of the spirit, a problem of life, a problem of culture.[81]

Economic progress depends on the spirit of the people manifest in their energized wills. Liang claimed that this stands opposed to the Western view that the objective world of economics controls life.

Other Voices

Some of China's most distinguished Western-trained philosophers have not perpetuated the style of investigation I have been describing. I include here Hu Shi, Jin Yuelin (a student of Bertrand Russell), and Feng Youlan. The same is true of many leading liberal educators, such as Cai Yuanpei, Jiang Menglin, Jiang Tingfu, and Fu Sinian. But other major non-Marxists, philosophers and theoreticians make the old Confucian concepts an important part of their doctrines.

In the 1930s and 1940s, the belief in the cause-effect relationship between rectifying minds and practical success was not yet a dominant theme among the most influential Marxist writers. That development awaited a shift in Mao's thought back to deep-seated Confucian themes, beginning in the 1950s. Writing in 1943, the Communist Party theoretician Ai Siqi identified the core problem in Chiang Kai-shek's philosophy in a spirit similar to the argument presented above.[82] He said that it causes the analyst to ignore the objective situation in favor of the minds of the people in it, and in this way, it obstructs the accumulation of complete knowledge. Ai described his difference with Chiang in these terms: Where Chiang said that the work of establishing the nation begins with the mind, Ai held that it begins with the correction of corruption and rectifying damage to the economy caused by landlords and capitalists.

Ominously, however, Ai never passed from his well-aimed critique to building a theoretically solid epistemology that could serve the sciences. He accepted, without defense, the existence of nonempirical first principles that explain social problems: economically based historical materialism, the necessity of transformed class relations to solving social problems, and the need for a strong revolutionary class. Like Sun Yat-sen and Chiang, he locates higher knowledge (*zhi*) in an elite where it dwells as "theory," while mere "perception" is manifest in the words of the masses. As I have noted, this denigrates technical skill. As Hu Shi noted, it splits knowledge and action, which are really interdependent. Finally, Ai did not consider how leaders' prejudices can alter the facts revealed by the masses as they formulate theory. Therefore he ignores the problem of controlling for investigator biases.

In the absence of such an epistemological foundation and its acceptance among Chinese Marxists, it was easy for the Maoist shift to earlier styles of inquiry to occur. The pre-1949 mass line principles were supposed to guarantee study of objective conditions at the local level. However, the elite nature of theory, the special truths to which only the elite has access, and the absence of controls over leadership relations with the masses in social investigation helped to open the door to a new florescence of old concepts. Correct ideas, in the leaders' minds, or as transmitted to the population through models, retained a status that overshadowed that of rigorous scientific research. This issue is the topic of the next chapter.

Consequences of the Confucian Style of Inquiry

Sun Yat-sen, Chiang Kai-shek, and many of China's most distinguished philosophers concurred on what is primary in the investigation of and proposed solutions to social problems. In their different ways, they asserted the same imperatives: Prize models from the nineteenth century and earlier, and investigate the minds of the people involved in problems. The most direct consequence was the shift of attention away from variables that were the actual agents of change in the years from the 1911 revolution until the Communist victory in 1949. Let me give an example to illustrate this point.

The traditional rural leadership had begun losing its legitimacy during the years of the Taiping Rebellion (1850–1864). Already tainted in some areas by humiliation at the hands of foreign powers, the rural gentry also lacked the modern education necessary to run the civil government in cities where many of their class had been lured by Chiang Kai-shek. Chiang, who was quite receptive to solving problems with technical skills such as those gained from the 1936 cooperative agreement with Germany (skills that would be used so effectively in the economic rebuilding of Taiwan after 1949), encouraged the gentry simply to copy the nineteenth-century Confucian Generals and Sun Yat-sen.

But the gentry officials in the countryside did not possess the modernization vision that Chinese youth and urban intellectuals longed for, nor were they trained to formulate a vision of society that differed from the old models. As a result, there was a vacuum of leadership in rural areas and little knowledge in the hands of central government about conditions there. When the Nationalists lost what little control they had in the countryside to the Communists, it was due, in part, to the fact that the Communists had undertaken empirical studies of actual local conditions. In the end, armed with detailed information, it was they who succeeded in introducing a political-administrative organization that effectively replaced the old gentry-dominated structures.[83]

CHAPTER THREE

Three Modern Models

A practitioner of the old style of inquiry looks for a model, in part as a means of rectifying the minds of participants, and in part as offering procedures to copy in solving the problem. This model may be a person or an organization. In practice, the selection of models for a given problem is haphazard. There is often no attempt to select a model that matches in specific details the person or situation with the problem. Further, the use a model may obscure consideration of facts that, if recognized, would immediately suggest the lack of fit between model and the situation to which it is being applied.

This chapter will be devoted to illustrating this process in recent Chinese history. While I could simply point to three general models to do this, it may be more instructive to single out specific instances of their application to particular movements or events. The purpose of these examples is to show the reach of general models and identify the ways in which they distort inquiry. The models I will discuss include: first, the Yan'an-centered society of the guerrilla period (late 1930s and 1940s), which was popular from the late 1950s into the 1980s, spanning the Mao and Deng eras. The second is the Soviet Union, a model derived from a foreign socialist society, popular in the early 1950s. Finally, there is the Daqing oil fields, a model of industrial organization for society as a whole.

When we think of the old style of inquiry in modern China, we usually think of Mao Zedong's rapid agricultural collectivization policy, his Great Leap Forward, and his Cultural Revolution of the 1950s and 1960s. There is nothing wrong with this, but I will touch only superficially on the details of these events, because they are so well-known.

I want to devote these pages to showing that matters were, in fact, more complex than they have seemed. First, I want to point out that the pre-1949 Mao manifested a mixture of interest in the old mind-rectification idea, and perhaps less appreciated by Chinese and Western scholars, some degree of respect for objective investigation. A decade after the Communist victory the latter interest nearly vanishes. A more traditional methodology, concern with the content of minds and interest in copying models, increasingly dominates inquiry. Second, I want to underscore that the impact of this old style of inquiry both predates and extends well beyond those two famous movements, the Great Leap (and its predecessor, agricultural collectivization) and the Cultural Revolution. Finally, by giving two examples that date from the period after the death of Mao, I can once again emphasize the point already made in the previous chapter—that recent evidence of the "residue" of traditional inquiry methods can be found not only in the practices of the Chairman.

There are slogans in Mao's speeches and writings from 1939–1945, that stress the obligation to be objective in inquiry: "If there has been no investigation, one does not have the right to speak."[1] "In investigating questions of fact one must first have detailed source material."[2] But this was more than sloganeering. The frequency and range of topics addressed with comments like these indicate that before the 1949 victory, Mao had a real depth of commitment to avoiding the old style of inquiry and its easy solutions.

A selection from 1941 shows him rejecting people whose designs for social change were not derived from objective conditions: "They only have some subjective wish to transform the world or to transform China or to transform north China or to transform the cities, and they do not have a sound design. Their designs are not scientific, but subjective and muddled."[3] He said that he was always grasping new facts and acquiring new knowledge, as though to turn aside the fixed theses that characterize any orthodoxy. There were no universal solutions to problems, good for all time and places: "And also, for many questions, one must personally go down to the countryside. Only then can one come to an understanding; according to the different actual objects and conditions, there will be [different] solutions."[4] By 1945 he had at least partly undercut the claim that there is a hierarchy of knowers who are infallible because of their access to basic truths: "Concerning having made mistakes, it is not just one or two persons who do this. Everyone makes mistakes. I have also made mistakes. . . . In fact, in my work of the past twenty-some years, whether in military matters, politics, or party work, I have made mistakes in all of them."[5]

The very concept of "people's war" that evolved during the 1930s was a mixture of concern with objectivity *and* with the old style of problem solving. It was a doctrine that insisted on objective facts or reports from the field as the basis of tactics. On the basis of facts, the commander decides whether or not he can win, and he never fights unless he believes he can. Simultaneously, however, this same Mao retained the old belief in the power of people armed with ideas to transform the objective social world according to their ideals.[6] As Maurice Meisner has shown, the Long March experience reinforced this belief.

The classical tradition of strength based on winning the people's minds in *Mencius, Xunzi,* and *Laozi* introduced another, older dimension into the revolutionary struggle. The early legacy, developed over two thousand years ago, held that a ruler with a virtuous character, but lacking weapons and a large population, can ultimately triumph over the objectively strong but oppressive ruler. This is a good point to pause and remember that mind sometimes does prevail over matter, that objectively weak but highly motivated guerrillas movements can triumph, as the United States learned in Vietnam. The problem arises when only will, or inquiry directed solely by social values, supports an effort at change. The "people's war" was carried by both—popular willpower and objective inquiry.

Since these two perspectives coexisted in pre-1949 China, the result was respect for a highly motivated populace combined with attention to the details of specific conditions where the population might have to act. This was a powerful combination. But if the investigation of things had become merely a slogan, leaving the old style of inquiry as the only tool for tackling problems, the result would probably have been unfortunate. Slippage between a model and the situation at hand is bound to occur where there is no interest in the particulars of the situation and mind rectification takes the place of fact gathering. A reversion to the old style indeed did happened after 1949. However, there has never been a return to the simplicity of a single model or the complete repudiation of objectivity among elites.

The most obvious reason for the reversion to the old style of inquiry was that it was congenial to the authoritarian political system Communist leaders wished to impose. Establishing models for people to emulate in effect tells them to ignore their own judgment and follow the antecedent authority of the model. Another reason for the reversion was the emphasis traditional inquiry places on the possibilities of willpower. Thus, it provided a boost for rapid modernization, remaining useful to leaders who compared China's economic conditions to those of the Western nations and to the U.S.S.R.

The Yan'an Model

There were important premises about knowledge consistent with the old style of inquiry that developed during the guerrilla period and endured after the Communist victory. These include the idea of a hierarchy of knowledge. With it, of course, went the justification for entitling leaders to control other people because of their exclusive access to higher level knowledge, namely, "rational knowledge" or theory. This set up a situation where the scope of legitimate inquiry shrank as certain forms of direct experience were reduced to the status of mere "perception."

The basics of the new elite theory do date from Mao Zedong's pre-victory works "On Practice" and "On Methods of Leadership." In fact, the latter essay explicitly draws together guerrilla-inspired notions about leadership and a theory of knowledge. This theory contends that in learning, an individual performs "practice"—purposively acts in the environment—which generates perceptions. Reflection then occurs in his mind through which he formulates theories (that is, hypotheses) based on those perceptions. He then applies his theories to subsequent practice. This is a continuous cycle, whereby a hypothesis is constantly revised and practice improved. By analogy, leaders work with or talk to ordinary people, gaining ideas in a way similar to the "practice" phase for the individual. They then return to their offices to transform what they learned from the masses into systematic theory (policy). This is parallel to the conceptualizing process of the individual. Finally, they then turn around and instruct the people in their policy, and the people are expected to incorporate that policy into their own "practice"—a process whose result should be similar to that of an individual testing a hypothesis. Mao spelled out the relation between epistemology and the function of leaders in this passage:

> In all the practical work of our Party, all correct leadership is necessarily "from the masses, to the masses." This means: take the ideas of the masses (scattered and unsystematic ideas) and concentrate them (through study turn them into concentrated and systematic ideas), then go to the masses and propagate and explain these ideas until the masses embrace them as their own, hold fast to them, and translate them into action, and test the correctness of these ideas in such action.... Such is the Marxist theory of knowledge.[7]

Thus, there were two agents in Mao's old-style solution to post-1949 problems. Leaders, possessors of the upright minds and cognitive understanding of China's historical goals, were the vanguard. The leaders taught the Chinese people what to do to achieve goals, thereby turning their minds, especially those of the peasantry, into the other agent.

The Maoist approach was manifest in three different events. These reflected the Yan'an model, though they were preceded by a period in which the Soviet model dominated (1949–1955). The three movements were agricultural collectiviztion, the Great Leap Forward, and the Cultural Revolution. I introduce these movements by noting that Mao had complex psychological motives in addition to his reflexive reliance on the old style of problem solving for filtering out facts uncongenial to his goals or methods. As reported by his doctor, he tended to see conspiracies everywhere.[8] He rejected facts, claiming they had been cooked up or contrived by those seeking to erode his power. As for lower level officials, it was fear for their own lives or careers that led to their lying about meeting or exceeding production targets during the agricultural movement and Great Leap.[9]

Thus, the very same Mao who said that leaders should "take the ideas of the masses" and "seek truth from facts" did not observe these guidelines during the movements of the 1950s and 1960s. Other high officials, however, were more cautious and criticized Mao's economic policies in *People's Daily* editorials and elsewhere. Not all leaders were enamored with his method of problem solving.[10]

The first movement to reflect the Yan'an model, agricultural collectivization, began in late 1955. Relying on political education to transform the peasants' attitudes, and sometimes, coercive organization by cadres, Mao attempted to achieve rapid consolidation of individual family farms into agricultural cooperatives. With faith in the power of mind rectification, Mao overrode Party goals concerning both the number of farms to be affected and the dates by which the targets would be met. He brushed aside high-level opposition and sought support from provincial and local-level leaders instead. Full socialist collectivization was achieved throughout China by early 1957, over two years ahead of schedule.[11] A manifesto that fully reveals Mao's old-style faith is his 1956 work, *Socialist Upsurge in the Chinese Countryside.*[12]

These cooperatives were precursors to the communes, which were developed during the second critical movement, the Great Leap Forward (1958–1960). China had limited resources, but it could not repeat the strategy of the First Five-Year Plan, squeezing even more capital from the agricultural sector to pay for heavy industry. Instead, social reorganization would have to provide the means to support industrialization. Thousands of peasants from different villages were formed into "production brigades," and those in turn were grouped into communes. The economic goal of the Maoist policy was still rapid industrialization and relieving urban unemployment; its social goal was to eliminate urban-rural and mental-manual distinctions, thereby achieving the status egalitarianism that Mao associated with Yan'an. The means to achieve his goals were ideological training to teach people correct thinking, the development of communes to provide the organizational setting for concentrated labor and for changing peasant minds into communist minds, and slack time use of peasant labor to build small-scale industry.

But the years of the Great Leap Forward witnessed severe weather and the canceling of Soviet technical aid. Both contributed to the catastrophes associated with that movement, but there were other reasons for its failure inherent to the movement itself. Fearful of expectations demanded by their superiors, officials at the local level lied about production output, inflating it in their reports. The state then demanded more grain from the farmers. The long-term economic cost of these cooperatives and communes included reduced individual and individual family incentives for agricultural productivity. In addition, starvation followed the reduced productivity and reduced supplies of food after the government had helped itself. In the early 1980s, peasants actively destroyed the cooperative granaries that were symbols of that movement. The small-scale industry of the time included, of course, the infamously flawed backyard blast furnaces. The problem with this initiative was that Mao had filtered out facts about steel needing to be produced in modern plants. Instead, he favored using backyard furnaces that were fed in part with the farmers' pots and pans. Another cost, then, was the waste of resources involved in these rural industrialization projects—melting down metal tools and food preparation equipment to make steel, for example.

Influenced by the Maoist mind-over-matter approach to solving problems in the rapid transformation of the economy and society, Liu Shaoqi put forth a slogan that epitomized the spirit of these first two movements: "Go all-out, aim high, and build socialism with greater, faster, better, and more economical results." Soon another slogan joined the first: "Man is the decisive factor" (in any objective situation). This meant that ideas, not the objective conditions, were crucial in success or failure. Another slogan, "politics in command," meant that there were no social, cultural, or economic issues immune from guidance by moral or political considerations.

Mao had several goals in instigating the third movement, the Cultural Revolution. In addition to personal revenge against perceived enemies within the Party, these included destroying advocates of market incentives within the Party, shaking up an elitist bureaucracy, steeling China for possible confrontation with the U.S. or U.S.S.R., and getting rid of customs from either the old society or from the West. The political goal that figured most prominently, however, was to accelerate the arrival of a socialist society made up of Chinese people armed with egalitarian and collectivist values.

The gradualistic requirements of the materialist conception of history could be ignored as the mind-transforming agents of change telescoped China's development. Consistent with the traditions of the old style of inquiry, when faced with a pressing economic or social problem, the leadership went to work on the minds of the people. Thus, the primary and secondary schools closed for three to four years, universities for five or more years, so that the modes of teaching and student recruitment could be changed. Increasingly anarchic bands of young political educators roamed the country mixing education and bully tactics and an entire generation lost its opportunity for formal education. Neighbors took revenge against neighbors for perceived grievances, justifying their revenge as being in line with the model of Mao himself. That is, they claimed political rectitude while beating up supposed political enemies.

A common theme in agricultural collectivization, the Great Leap Forward, and the Cultural Revolution was the psychological motivation of individual Chinese for economic modernization. My description of the Maoist approach has focused on the egalitarian social organization and changing the people's minds so that their actions stemmed from commitment to certain social values. The focus on changing the minds of the people persisted in the reversion by some leaders to the Yan'an model, even after Mao's death.

Writing in the 1960s, Mao revealed the importance of the Yan'an model in the matter of individual motivation. He was opposing an obvious competing candidate for motivation, namely material incentives in the form of wide salary differentials.

> When we were in the base areas [the years of guerrilla warfare], we enforced a free supply system. People were a little healthier then. They did not quarrel on account of going after wages. After liberation, we instituted a wage system and arranged all personnel in order of rank. On the contrary, more troubles arose. Many people frequently quarreled in their fight for a higher rank. As a result, this necessitated a lot of persuading.
>
> Ours is a party which had engaged in more than twenty years of continuous war. We enforced a free supply system over a long period.... Right up to the early stages of liberation, people on the whole lived an egalitarian life. They worked hard and fought bravely on the battlefield. They absolutely did not rely on material incentive for encouragement, but on revolutionary spirit.[13]

The free-supply system, in lieu of salaries, remained in effect until 1954. Mao is reported to have wanted to reestablish it in rural communes in 1958.[14] In the passage above Mao does not consider the fact that procedures of a simple society may not work in a complex society covering vast areas and numbers of people with all their regional variations. In short, the model was not a proper fit with China's social situation of the 1950s and 1960s when the Communist Party leaders were running the entire country. This represents a reversal of the position Mao had taken on the cusp of victory. In a 1949 speech at the Second Plenum of the Seventh Central Committee, he said that he was learning from the Soviet Union and from the Kuomintang holdovers about how to organize China's cities for a new era. By 1958 he had abandoned the idea of new ways for a new era for the old style of problem solving, using the Yan'an experience as his model.

This model did not die with Mao, and I now turn to my principal illustration of it. The Yan'an model survived well into the Deng era, and the point of the following example is to show how the old style of inuiry persisted beyond Mao himself. During the winter of 1983, the Central Committee of the Chinese Communist Party identified widespread corruption within the membership of the Party. Members were violating fiscal and economic regulations, ruining national plans, retaining for local use tax income due the central government, concocting pretexts for their illegal activities, and squandering resources. In their own districts, they were adjusting wages upward and obtaining jobs for their family and friends. They were said to manifest no compassion for the troubles of the masses.[15]

The Central Committee assigned then General Secretary Hu Yaobang the task of leading a party-wide campaign to rectify this situation. The Committee document explaining the conditions requiring this move described the method for realizing that goal:

> After the promulgation of this decision [concerning rectification], all Party units must organize their members to study carefully the materials for the rectification of the Party selected by the Central Committee. Thereby they will heighten the members' ideological consciousness [*sixiang juewu*] and strengthen the units' vitality.... Our basic methodology for rectifying the Party this time is [this]: after careful study of the materials and having raised their ideological consciousness, the Party members must initiate criticism and self-criticism, in order to distinguish right from wrong, to correct mistakes, and to purify their organizations. Throughout the process of rectification, from beginning to end, we must strengthen ideological education, and focus on heightening and broadening ideological consciousness.[16]

Another essay of the time refers to new economic policies, the open door to the West, and new political, cultural, and educational policies. It says that "The ability to carry out [such] a policy depends on ideological work being propagandized."[17]

The major Central Committee document has the flavor of something written during the Yan'an guerrilla days of the late 1930s and 1940s.

There are references to applying the mass-line style of work within the Party and externally using a work style marked by direct cadre consultation with villagers.[18] Indeed, there is evidence in the document's conclusion that those who wrote it had in mind the Yan'an model: "During its long revolutionary struggle, our Party has had an excellent tradition of using the promulgation of ideology as foremost in strengthening the hold of the Party."[19] The point is not that Hu's only approach to problem solving involved copying the Yan'an model; it is that this approach coexisted with others.

Contrary to the expectation of its formulators, but consistent with my critique of the use of models, the Rectification Campaign was followed by even worse forms and levels of corruption than those that had precipitated it in the first place. These were reported to include cadres in the Party, the government, the army, and schools importing cars for personal use or profit, openly demanding bribes, and so forth.[20]

The same configuration of factors that existed in the previous cases prevail here. The use of an inappropriate organizational model, coupled with a faith in attitudinal transformation, served to obscure crucial facts about the problems of the situation. Major facts that were ignored included the very different motivations of Party members in the guerrilla period and the 1980s. The guerrilla period required party members to remain incorrupt not simply "to be a good communist" but also for reasons of personal survival in the face of real dangers presented by the KMT and the Japanese. Through their upright demeanor they retained the good will of the peasants, who provided their logistical and intelligence needs. During the 1980s, these dangers no longer existed, making incorruptibility less than imperative. It was a different world, with new temptations from Western contacts to boot.

Deng Xiaoping did not routinely follow the old style of inquiry, however. He is correctly remembered for saying that it does not matter if a cat is white or black so long as it can catch a mouse, seeming to denigrate political values and elevate technical skills.

But there are traces of the Confucian inquiry even in his political biography. Some of his writings, reissued in June, 1983, helped set the tone for the abortive campaign described above. Those writings contain the observation that when we speak of improving Party leaders, it is most important to intensify ideological and political work. Also,

> In wishing to establish a socialist country, we not only want to have a high level of material civilization, but also a high level of spiritual civilization. So-called spiritual civilization does not refer only to education, science, culture (these are entirely necessary); it also refers to communist thought, ideals, beliefs, morality, discipline, revolutionary perspective on the world

> and principles, a comradely style of relations between people, and so forth.[21]

Deng Xiaoping, though symbolizing a new era, still played an indirect role in perpetuating the inappropriate Yan'an model. He did away with mass mobilization projects, the obsession with status egalitarianism, and the preference for the all-around generalist of the Yan'an days, as opposed to the specialist valued in modern industrial societies. Still, the fact that he, too, has relied on the idea of rectification suggests that when modernization efforts run into problems, there may well be a return to earlier ways, in which will is the primary vehicle for problem solving.

The Soviet Model

Although Mao had said, "Learn from the Soviet Union," by 1957 and 1958 he attacked Party officials for mindlessly imitating the U.S.S.R. and for treating the works of Marx like cookbook recipes.[22] His physician at the time reported him as saying, "I want to learn from the United States."[23] But the Soviet model made a powerful impact, especially during the early 1950s.

The best-known application of the Soviet model was the First Five-Year Plan, mentioned above. But there is another example that is not generally known to be linked to the Soviet model. This is a case involving population planning. It manifests all the traits of the old Confucian style of inquiry.

In 1953 the Chinese government carried out a nationwide census that produced the figure 601,938,035 for China's population as of June 30 of that year. It was estimated that the population would increase by twelve to thirteen million each year, a rate of 2 percent. In Shanghai the rate was 3.9 percent per year.[24]

Ma Yinchu was a social scientist of some stature, president of Peking University and a member of the National People's Congress. Studying the numbers, he guessed that the national rate of growth might actually be 3 percent. But even taking the lower percentage, he calculated that in fifteen years the population would reach 800,000,000.[25] Thinking through the relation between these figures and what he estimated to be China's rate of capital accumulation, he saw a contradiction: the rate of population growth imposed a burden on the capacity for accumulation that would impede China's development. Here was a possible social problem. He then set to work gathering facts that might reveal the actual parameters of the problem.

Three times during the three years 1953–55 he made field trips to Zhejiang province. He gathered material from Jiangxi, Shanxi, Shandong, Jiangsu, Shanghai, and Beijing as well. Ma interviewed peasants and cadres in cooperatives about births, marriages, and deaths. Predictably, he encountered the peasant bias in favor of siring many sons. He discovered that local governments were sloganeering in favor of rapid population growth.[26] The materials that he gathered concerned not only population increase but also food production and the development of cultural activities and education. He analyzed the data province by province, and then he turned to comparable data from other countries. This work went into a report entitled, "Controlling Population and Scientific Research," which he planned to put forward at the second session of the First National People's Congress.[27]

That report elicited criticisms to the effect that there could be no population problems in a socialist country. Unswayed, Ma developed his ideas into his major theoretical work on the subject, *The New Theory of Population* (*Xin renkou lun*), which was presented to the Fourth Session of the NPC in 1957.[28] This work made a number of general points: rural productivity cannot be raised dramatically in a short period, accumulated resources decrease with population increase, and this includes the per person share of foodstuffs.[29] It also included references to the empirical sources for the findings, such as the birth records for state cotton mills in Shanghai.

The key policy change suggested by his research findings was to control the quantity and to improve the quality of the population. He suggested these means: to continue the practice of taking a regular census and formulate a population control policy, to limit the rate of births, to improve the level of scientific knowledge among the people, and to encourage late marriage and contraception.[30] He proposed a two-child family and opposed abortion, claiming that it takes a life and is bad for the mother's health.[31]

Mao Zedong's 1958 reply to these goals and means was unequivocal:

> In addition to the leadership of the Party, the population of 600,000,000 has been a decisive factor [in our success]. The greater the population, the higher the enthusiasm [*reqi*] the people have, and the stronger their vigor.[32]

Liu Shaoqi echoed this criticism, using the same language about the efficacy of properly aroused minds:

> The essence of this thinking is that it underestimates the [enthusiasm] of the organized revolutionary peasants in our country. Therefore it cannot but receive our *factual* [emphasis mine] refutation.[33]

A common theme in many of the criticisms was that "having many people is a good thing" (*ren duo shi hao shi*) according to an important law of historical materialism. Another is that Ma's thesis, focusing on humans as consumers rather than as producers, treats them as enemies. Following the attacks on him, Ma was removed from his position as president of Peking University. He lost his membership on the Standing Committee of the National People's Congress and was thrown into the Chinese gulag.

The critiques by these leaders and by others consistently ignored the empirically based reasoning in Ma's essay in favor of two other models. One model was the plan governing the first five years of the "revolutionary" regime, which took no account of the possible negative consequences of the demographic trajectory. This was a period of growth in agricultural productivity and in construction. Ma's critics inferred that the progress in levels of output would continue or increase, turning a blind eye to variables that might alter the situation in subsequent years.[34]

It has seldom been noted that Ma's critics repeatedly refer to the U.S.S.R. in their arguments. It was a model of a socialist country that succeeded economically while promoting population increase in the years after World War II. The Soviets had outlawed abortion in 1936, and in 1944 they introduced rewards for fertile mothers, and punishments in the form of taxes on the childless to promote population growth.[35] Specifically, Ma's critics wrote that the Soviet Union was approaching communism rapidly, was automating its production processes, and was overtaking the United States in its average per capita production output. All of these wonders came about without a population control policy. The U.S.S.R. was a model of social value (the rapid advance of communism) and economic value (automation and an output outpacing that of the U.S.).

In addition to the point that the wonders they attributed to the U.S.S.R. were themselves unsubstantiated, the Chinese critics of Ma Yinchu ignored the factual differences between the two countries, not the least of which was the portion of the total population lost by the U.S.S.R. in the war.[36] These critics rested their case with the expectation that psychological "enthusiasm" generated by copying the minds of the Soviets and of the Chinese themselves during the first five years of Party rule, guaranteed that resources would outpace population growth. In addition, the assumed ethical "superiority" of Soviet procedures (policies involving laws and clinics that ignore population planning) blinded the Chinese critics to the need to review all sorts of relevant facts.

None of this is to claim that Ma's own data were flawless. Indeed, like Malthus, he did not figure in how technical development could positively increase China's productivity. The point, however, is the way in which Ma was refuted and his data ignored.

Years later, many of Ma's facts were found to be relevant. On September 14, 1979, the Central Committee of the Chinese Communist Party reversed its resolution of twenty years before that had condemned Ma Yinchu. It said, "Mr. Ma Yinchu's 'New Theory of Population' viewpoint was correct, and the various things he advocated can be implemented."[37] Noting the heavy burden that this population growth would continue to put on China's development, the author of Ma's 1986 biography wrote that had his analysis been accepted, the population would have been smaller by 250,000,000.

Obviously, in addition to their faith in the "enthusiasm" of the people, the leaders held beliefs that they also proselytized to those people. These included the idea that taking the U.S.S.R. as analogous to China, and the first five years of the Communist government as analogous to any future five-year period, was the way to go about solving China's problems. Matters of belief and enthusiasm went together. Belief about the appropriateness of models that were in fact inappropriate effectively masked many relevant facts, which were then ignored.

The Daqing Model

Bohai No. 2 was the name of an offshore drilling platform that had been purchased from abroad at considerable expense in 1973. In November 1979, the platform was being towed from a previous drilling site to a new one in the Gulf of the Bohai off China's northeast coast. According to the rules of the Ministry of Petroleum, the team on the platform was to have fifteen days prior to a move to a new site to prepare for the move. According to the same rules, the team should receive from the Ministry accurate information about water depth, underwater land formations, and the thickness of the bottom sediment.[38] In addition, the officials ashore were to forward to the platform crew all current meteorological information. The platform team did its job properly, sending to headquarters three reports outlining specific problems they were encountering, and emphasizing their need for the facts just described.

Disregarding standard procedures, the Ministry ordered the team to prepare for the move in four days, rather than fifteen. It ignored the rules concerning finding and furnishing the facts about water, sediment, and weather conditions, and in fact did not furnish any of the usual information. The team's reports were disregarded.[39] In addition to ignoring circumstantial information, we will see that the administrators in charge of the project were actually imitating a model, the Daqing model, and disregarded the differences between it and conditions at the Bohai No. 2 platform. These administrative decisions and practices led to disaster, with loss of life and significant political consequences.

In 1979 the inland Daqing oil fields in Heilongjiang Province still served as a model for industrial production, just as Dazhai did for farming. These units provided models of production processes and also demonstrated the miracles that a proper (patriotic) attitude toward goals could achieve. The officials in the Ministry of Petroleum who were in charge of Bohai No. 2 had taken Daqing as their model regardless of the fact that Daqing's operation bore little resemblance to oil platform production.

The Chinese people knew about Daqing from, among other things, the catchy phrases used to describe it and its personnel. These found their way into the discussions of Bohai No. 2.[40] There were expressions that referred to a production process model and also to model workers with rectified minds. These individuals, such as "the industrial man" Wang Tieren, the chief human model at Daqing, were described as "having a dashing spirit" (*you ruiqi*) and "having enthusiasm" (*you ganjin*), to convey the point that they paid no attention to a bad situation. However, should someone ask about the objective facts of a situation, he was said to "lack enthusiasm."[41]

It was reassuring to the administrators of the Gulf of Bohai oil production to have such a model toward the end of October 1979, because with the winter freeze in sight, they were short of their production target of 20 million tons for the season. When specialists raised problems at No. 2, the administrators could take comfort in the fact that things had been even worse in the early years at Daqing. They knew that those difficulties had been overcome because of the upright minds of the workers and officials there.

In the early morning of November 25, 1979, under the impact of a force-ten wind, Bohai No. 2 capsized, drowning 72 of the 74 team members aboard and destroying the enormous investment in the platform itself. Vice-Premier Kang Shi'en, in charge of the petroleum industry, was reprimanded. The Minister of the Petroleum Industry was dismissed, and some officials directly responsible in the Bureau of Ocean Petroleum Prospecting were prosecuted.

In his self-criticism, the dismissed minister stated that the cause of the tragedy was "being prejudiced in favor of the subjective, and exaggerating subjective initiative" (*kuada zhuguan nengdongxing*). He said that "subjective will replaced objective reality" (*zhuguan yizhi daiti keguan shiji*) and that administrators had made plans that ran counter to objective possibilities. He said that people had "treated respect for science and for doing things according to objective laws as 'fearing difficulty'."[42] Other assessments spoke of "not respecting science, paying no attention to actual conditions, going against objective laws, and ignoring the correct opinions of the masses and of specialists."[43]

The consequences of reliance on models and the priority of inner attitudinal propriety at Bohai No. 2 were extremely costly to the Chinese government, the workers, and the nation. A *People's Daily* editorial of August 1980, went so far as to directly state that the problem lay with the Petroleum Ministry's copying old modes of action and not paying attention to what was different about the Bohai case: the machinery was new and like nothing at Daqing, and the work was taking place at sea, not on land.[44] Confidence in "subjective initiative" had facilitated the dismissal of these obvious and critical facts.

Opportunities for Change

But there was a movement afoot that challenged the inflated expectations of a properly armed mind. It began in 1978, mounted by such intellectuals and trouble makers for the Party as Wang Ruoshui and Yang Xianzhen. Its blossoming and failure have been nicely documented by Kalpana Misra. She cites a well-formulated attack on the residues of the old style of inquiry in Maoism, published in 1980. It criticizes the tendency that we saw in the 1930s to give subjective content to the term "practice," such that only morally or politically goal-directed actions are worthy of the name. These moral-political goals reduce the scope of operations, and hence the range of pertinent facts in any inquiry about the objective world. They manifest a continued failure to differentiate the subjective and objective realms, or what in Confucian terms are the realms of humans and heaven. This is the position of Mr. Ze Ming, in his article, "Refutation of 'Practice is the Only Source of Knowledge'":

> Not all subjective knowledge can be transformed into direct reality.... Twenty years ago, it was promulgated that by 1967 the grain output would be 400-600 *jin* per worker, that in 10 or 15 years, we would be entering communism, that mechanization of agriculture would be completed in 10

> years—all this was "subjective knowledge," and all excellent wishes and aims, but it did not become direct reality although the country worked hard for it. This proves completely that the aim which subjective knowledge bestows on practice must be produced from the objective world, and cannot be fixed subjectively. . . .[45]

This was a theoretical attack on an aspect of the old manner of dealing with problems. It failed to gain any official acceptance.

Maoists exaggerated the ability of proletarians and peasants armed with the correct class consciousness to leap over objective economic backwardness and telescope the arrival of a new historical stage. Dr. Misra explains the failure of the movement against that exaggeration by saying that the legitimacy of the rulers of China depends in part on their claim to represent progressive classes armed with the correct consciousness that have moved China into the socialist stage. To attack mind-over-matter voluntarism, she says, is to undercut that legitimacy.

Doubtless there is validity to this interpretation. At the same time, my own thesis leads to the conclusion that any reformist attack on the old style of inquiry would also fail because this inquiry is such a deeply ingrained part of elite Chinese culture. It differs qualitatively from the German and Russian Marxist notions of permanent revolution that center exclusively on the revolutionary action of classes and class leaders. It differs in that the Confucian style of approaching problems has always included the epistemological considerations of the role of models and views about the narrow nature of knowledge, which in the modern period have often clustered around the term "practice."

Fortunately there are two glimmers of hope on the horizon which I will deal with in detail in chapters 4 and 5. One concerns the denial of the union of humans and heaven or the union of subjective and objective worlds. It backs away from the stand that human values such as hierarchy and role relationships pervade everything. This opportunity for a shift in inquiry is also embedded in popular culture. I will illustrate this with the work of a popular playwright who delightfully attacks the transformation of a scientific study into a study of the role relations of the investigators. Thus, the impetus for a shift in inquiry styles comes from many directions; professional theorists are not its only source. As a result, this shift is perhaps more likely to succeed.

But there is a second opportunity for change, a chance to combat the use of models that instill a kind of uniformity of thought. That opportunity lies with the emergence of the value of individual autonomy in China. Unlike the reformist theoreticians' direct attack on the power of the mind, this development arises mainly from popular culture. To enhance this value is to deflate the reflexive reliance on the external authority embodied in models. It legitimizes individual judgment. This is not the same as placing value on individualism in the sense of glorifying a plurality of thousands upon thousands of discrete perspectives. Inquiry anywhere is an activity conducted by groups of people, not by individuals.[46] This is even more true in China with its social traditions. Certainly the perspective of Ma Yinchu was shared by all of his field research assistants. Many of the technicians connected with the Bohai No. 2 platform had demanded facts about sediment, currents, and weather. In the long run and practically speaking, their attitudes and actions in some sense validate the individual mind as a legitimate arbiter of what is true and false and of the values that motivate action. This is not the same as pursuing multiplicity for its own sake.

As I will show in the final chapter, there is abundant evidence that the value of individual autonomy has been gaining strength in China. However, as I will argue in the next chapter, acceptance of individual autonomy in judgment and a turn away from traditional model emulation is not in itself sufficient to satisfy the conditions for objective inquiry. There must also exist the opportunity for unfettered criticism of hypotheses, evidence, and inferences from that evidence. In this regard, matters remain in flux.

CHAPTER FOUR

The Emergence of Objectivity in Modern Chinese Inquiry

The movements I am about to describe have their roots in the activities of two different groups of Chinese in the 1930s and 1940s. One was made up of liberal educators who held the model of Western science in great esteem, though they themselves were not scientists. The other included the second generation of Chinese scientists working in China. Though shying away from political involvement, these scientists helped to create an awareness in the urban areas of objective inquiry, that is, inquiry not directed by political values. They did so through the example of their own research and the impact it made on the institutions in which they worked. Much of their story which I will summarize below has been documented in the studies of D.W.Y. Kwok and James Reardon-Anderson.

Precursors to Change

The liberal educators calling for changes included Cai Yuanpei, an aesthetician and former president of Peking University; Jiang Menglin, an educator; the historians Jiang Tingfu and Fu Sinian; and the philosopher Hu Shi.[1] Their shared stance repudiated the realm of immaterial spirit, prized the scientific method as the source of all truth, accepted the deterministic and predictable relations of physical cause and effect, and affirmed confidence in progress to a utopian future.[2]

Their primary contribution toward establishing a new style of inquiry was to promote an ideal. That ideal entailed the pursuit of research and education free from political or religious control by authorities outside the laboratory or the academy. They held that the aim of study is the development of the individual, and this can only occur when external authorities do not intrude on or constrain the process of inquiry.[3]

These liberal educators and advocates of individual development were pitted against the Kuomintang right wing, which was invested in the doctrines of such figures as the philosopher Zhang Junmai and Chen

Lifu. This faction implemented the principles described in chapter 2, namely, that all activity must go forward under the guidance of moral or political values. This means that scientific inquiry, which deals with the material world, must be guided by a Chinese spirit of ethics.[4] One can assume that "ethical spirit" referred to the Three People's Principles as defined by the KMT leadership. Among other things, this meant promoting the "people's livelihood" through applied science. This program half succeeded. The Ministry of Education in Nanking did arrange to shift resources to the fields that met its standard of addressing what the government determined to be the practical needs of the Chinese people. This meant transferring money to courses in agriculture, industry, medicine, and commerce; it also meant taking money away from other fields. However, the development of the individual did not figure in any statements of KMT goals. To understand why the powerful conservatives were only half successful, we must turn to that other group that helped lay the foundation for a change in the practice of inquiry, the Chinese scientists.

By the mid 1930s, Chinese scientists were becoming well established in their institutions. They were performing productive research in laboratories at Tsinghua University, National Central University in Nanking, and at Zhejiang University, all government schools. Even National Peking University saw improvements in scientific research in this period. In part, the flourishing of science was a direct result of the Ministry of Education, controlled by conservatives who redirected resources to what they considered to be applied science. This was their "half success". The conservatives were unsuccessful to the extent that they were unable to control what went on in the universities and hospitals. Even within the Ministry there was opposition to those officials who favored blatant intrusion. So the scientists, by and large without interference, were able to offer courses similar to those of the European or American institutions where they had studied. They taught basic theory as well as applied subject matter.[5]

The lesson in all of this is that there was a delicate line between government support and government intrusion. Government financial resources played an extremely helpful role in promoting institutions that practiced scientific methodology, since their programs made that approach more widely known and accepted. Government intrusion would have meant that political values (in the Chinese case, short-term utility) might have altered the content of courses and thereby narrowed scientific inquiry to problems of applied technology. In the 1930s, the need to teach the scientific method or approach was considered more pressing than potential discoveries to be made. In the words of one practicing scientist at that time, "Promoting the research atmosphere and teaching research methods are more important, by far, than the results of the research itself."[6]

Enduring Obstacles

The ideal of objectivity that emerged in the 1930s was submerged during the Maoist years. These were the times of uniting the "red" and the "expert," and of "politics in command." In short, the Communists succeeded overwhelmingly in having their political and social values drive inquiry. Even after the death of Mao, there have been continued attempts to justify the intrusion of nonscientific values into the process of investigation. In short, there have been various barriers erected against objectivity.

These obstacles have come in several different forms. In the two decades since the death of Mao a principal barrier has been the assumption that human values derive from human needs. The relation between values and needs may have some vague and partial plausibility. However, the danger with it lies in the assertion that follows from it, namely, that the individual's own needs play a legitimate role in the determination of objective knowledge. This is the old habit of unifying humans and nature in a new guise.

At a theoretical level, Chinese scholarly journals are packed with murky studies making some variation of the claim that "the category of value is the basic category in epistemology." They never distinguish epistemic from social or moral values.[7] Their thrust is to assert that cognition always involves a combination of facts and values, especially the value of need satisfaction, and these values legitimately guide the selection of certain objective phenomena as targets of study.[8] Even where an author is likely to distinguish factual and value knowledge, he is likely to end up saying, "Truth has value; it is a union of the scientific and the normative."[9]

> What the scientific nature of truth reflects is a relation of truth with the objective; it is a reliable reflection of objective things and laws. It is correct. Its value nature reflects the relation of truth to the subject. It says that truth can satisfy a certain subject's need. It is useful.[10]

Here is a comparable statement that serves as our bridge to understanding why this matters: "In the practical process of knowing, the scientific and value elements often mix together."[11] The key word is "practical," a technical word that has some of the connotations of "operations" in Western philosophy. Among other things, it refers to the acts we carry out in trying to verify some theory or hypothesis. The author of a similar position puts it this way,

> Whether or not some knowledge or theory has any vitality rests on whether or not it serves practice, whether or not it fulfills some material or spiritual need of society (or a subject)."[12]

This means that theory-testing operations are not inspired by the objective situation but by the *needs* of the tester. They are goal-directed, when the goal concerns fulfilling certain kinds of subjective needs. Back in the 1930s, Chiang Kai-shek had defined practice as goal-directed action. In his words, *xing* (practice) is action that "has a certain goal and direction," and "is in accord with heavenly principles and human sentiments."[13] This definition of practice endures today. Such a view trivializes any random, exploratory acts. It privileges self-fulfilling actions that promise a quick pay-off according to someone's transitory "need." As one person described this dangerous thesis, the practical activity of the subject should not only be based on the "is" (*benlai ru ci*) of the social object but should also submit to the restriction of the "should" principle (*yingdang ru ci*).[14]

There is no better example of the intrusion of nonepistemic, subjective values into objective subject matter than the case of psychology. Lin Fang was a noted member of the Institute of Psychology in the Chinese Academy of Sciences until his death in the late 1980s. His work demonstrates the inheritance in modern dress of the Confucian penchant for projecting both hierarchy and goal-directedness onto an objective subject, human psychology. Lin attributed subjectively derived values to humans who were, in this case, considered objective phenomena, the target of study.

Hierarchy appears in his formulation of levels of worth within the animal kingdom—humans are of highest worth[15]—and also within the range of human motives.[16] Something like the desire "to create freely" and the *need* for self-actualization[17] rank near the top. This rank ordering clearly derives in part from Marx's early work, *Economic and Philosophical Manuscripts,* and from the work of the Western psychologist Maslow, whose hierarchy of human needs is well known. There is something familiar and appealing to those of us from certain cultural backgrounds about this kind of almost Platonic hierarchy. The problem is that neither Lin Fang nor Maslow ever explains the justification for the standard by which we determine motives to be high or low. The outside analyst can only infer that this is a case of taking a subjective standard or value in the individual writer's mind and assuming it applies to the objective topic of humans in general.

Lin Fang introduces a teleological element into psychology by saying that psychology should take how people can develop into "true persons" as its subject matter.[18] To develop in this way is the completion of the process of self-actualization.[19] Lin himself accepted the noble Confucian ideal of "being a complete person" (*zuo ren*) and attributed the process toward that goal to the human developmental structure, combining matters of fact and value in the same description. The potential for development to a higher level is built into humans from birth, a factual matter. Lin also asserted their obligation to complete that development, clearly a value issue.

Another leading figure whose ideas reflect this perspective is Pan Shu, who also died in the 1980s. Two of his positions are directly pertinent. One was that China's social scientists should build psychology as a field with Chinese characteristics. The aim should not be to contribute to the growth of an international or universal science of human behavior.[20] I infer from this position that material selected for study in a "psychology with Chinese characteristics" would be relevant to some politically preestablished values (or social "needs"), such as rapid industrialization. In addition to the patriotic interest in psychology with Chinese characteristics, in Pan's thinking, the official ideology of dialectical materialism also should guide inquiry. Pan wrote, "Actually, we always have a perspective on facts; if it is not materialistic, then it is idealistic, or sometimes it goes from one perspective to the other."[21] At the very least the materialist is required to stay away from the biological model, remember to emphasize how humans differ from other animals and the fact that they are of higher worth, and note that humans have a social nature (which includes ideological thinking) as well as a biological one and that the former is higher than the latter.

Intriguingly, but not unexpectedly, Pan Shu approved of the ancient premise that heaven, earth, and humans form a continuum. He maintained that this idea should guide the investigation of topics in psychology today.[22] So a psychology with Chinese characteristics would also draw on first principles from ancient Chinese cosmological thought such as the unity of heaven and humans.[23] Obstacles to objectivity, then, include not only the requirement that the test of a theory meet the subjective criterion of someone's need fulfillment. The attribution of subjectively derived values to objective targets of study also becomes a legitimate practice by virtue of the continued authority of traditional cosmology. For various reasons, this last obstacle has begun to be challenged.

A Theoretical Breakthrough

If the old style of inquiry limits the scope of relevant facts to those suggested by core social and political values, the key to breaking away from this approach is to separate the subjective (human) and objective (heavenly) realms. The assumed unity of the two has compelled the belief that their shared value traits were most worthy of study.

I do not have to worry about one of the traditional sources for belief in the old paradigm. That source is the claim that the innate structure of the mind (consisting of patterns both prescriptive and descriptive), if clarified, would be found to be identical to that of the entire natural world. I do not need to worry about this because thirty years of Maoism beat down quite hard on the idea that anything at all significant in human nature is innate. Although Maoist thinkers did not succeed in eradicating the idea of an innate moral sense, the old macrocosm-microcosm legacy (that patterns in the mind are duplicates of those in nature) seems defunct except in popular religious culture. The belief in mind magic is the real challenge. It is the legacy of failing to distinguish the subjective from the objective, which seems tied to the belief in "the unity of humans and heaven."

Happily, the call for a break with the idea of unity has been raised. A movement has emerged that includes a number of important writers from major institutions. By their redefinition of the terms "heaven" and "humans," they have tried to discredit the notion of unity. Now these terms are being equated with "objective world" and "subjective world," respectively. With the separation of heaven from humans, it becomes possible for the first time to consider nature in its own terms. In the last decades of this century, one of the pioneers in this breakthrough is Zhang Shiying, a professor of Western philosophy at Peking University, an undergraduate student of Feng Youlan and especially of He Lin, and a Hegel researcher. He writes,

> But the history of Chinese philosophy has excessively emphasized the unity of heaven and humans, emphasized the unified nature of things, and ignored the separation and opposition of the subjective and objective, ignored pluralism, individuation, ignored nature and natural science, ignored pure theoretical knowledge [such as how people know anything, or the form of knowing as opposed to its content] and the methodology of epistemology.[24]

This idea of Zhang's invites the objective world to reveal to us its full range of empirical characteristics, rather than imposing on it human traits.

It should be noted that there were pre-modern thinkers who made a distinction between what Westerners call the subjective and the objective. Wang Fuzhi (1619–1692) has one of the more intriguing takes on the matter. As Alison Black has shown, he strongly rejected reading human conceptions into nature. This includes his opposing the claim that nature has deliberate purposes. What we today call subjective, Wang would term "self-centered." Unlike many modern figures who distinguish the two realms, however, Wang treated irregularity as a trait of Nature and the attribution of uniformity to it as a self-centered human act. He meant that this involves taking a purely human concept and arrogantly assigning it to nature.[25] Wang's type of distinction did not gain a wide following in China.

Feng Youlan gets the credit for being one of the first in the modern era to lay out the idea that nature and humans should be understood as respectively the objective world of fact and the subjective world of human thought, emotion, and will. Back in the 1930s, in his *New Rationalistic Philosophy* (*Xin lixue*), Feng wrote "Knowledge and an [objective] realm are two totally different things. There is not necessarily a dependent relation between them."[26] There lurks in this claim a subjective-objective distinction (between a knower and a realm that he seeks to know).

One reason that Feng's contribution has remained obscure is that he also idealized the unity of humans and heaven. The confusion these positions generate may be cleared up once we realize that Feng characterized the world as consisting of two different realms, the "realm of truth" (*zhen ji*) and the "realm of actuality" (*shi ji*). The former is a transcendental realm, not of this world, and it is in this realm that the unity of heaven and humans is possible. But in the "realm of actuality," the subjective (human) and objective (heaven) separation is a fact and a necessary premise for inquiry. But even in the "realm of actuality," there are layers to his positions that must be peeled back so that the nuances are revealed.

Here is how unity applies to the "realm of truth," according to the *New Rationalistic Philosophy*. This unity is a matter of humans conceptualizing things as unified. Feng took the Neo-Confucian term *li*[b] (principle or pattern), which is both descriptive and prescriptive. He interpreted it as something similar to the "Platonic form" and the "universal". Descriptively, *li*[b] as "universal" involves the essential characteristics of a class of objects. For example, to have all angles combined equal 180 degrees and to have three sides is the essence of the class of objects known as triangles. Prescriptively, all members of a class *should* strive to live up to the standard or *li*[b] of their class; when they do, they are good. The fact-value fusion is built into the idea of *li*[b], so there is a *li*[b] of triangularity, just as there is a *li*[b] of the class humans. To introduce the notion of a class of things is to assume a unity among the many individual things. There are increasingly comprehensive classes, each with its *li*[b] (e.g., female, human, animal). Finally, there is the most comprehensive class of all, the class of "being" (*you*). The union of heaven and people occurs like this: All men and things, including each individual, are already parts of the whole. However, not all realize it or act in accordance with it, that is, with sympathy for other things. The more *li*[b], or universals, that are discovered, the more unity is brought to the diversity of the world. A person can potentially see things from the standpoint of heaven. He can transcend immediate experience because he brings all *li*[b] together in his mind conceptually, grasping the universals to which all things actually do conform. Thinking of everything in terms of a "great whole," is a spiritual state achieved through self-cultivation. It leads to comprehensive knowledge and manifests the unity of heaven and humans, a condition and a value consistently Confucian.

One of the enduring themes of this study has been the mixture of positions that coexist, even in the writings of single individuals. Feng is no exception. In some respects he is like the Confucian-inspired thinkers of chapter 2. The knowledge that he encouraged people to seek is not value-neutral. It is information that enhances our understanding of the meaning of life and that enables people to settle down and get on with the pursuit of living. This is "opening the mind." Developing a methodology for resolving scientific problems was not his goal. In fact, he attacked the Logical Positivists of Vienna for wanting to kill metaphysics.[27]

At the same time, there is an aspect of his views about the "realm of actuality" that was a precursor to the developments that began in the 1980s. The division that he made between the subjective and objective realms had an impact, even though his aim was not to solve scientific problems. He never abandoned his commitment to that division.

Feng's late writings, dating from the 1980s, lay out the modern equivalents for the old set of heaven and humans, which serve as background for making this subjective-objective distinction. He says that nature is what was called "heaven" in China's traditional philosophy; society and individuals are the so-called "human." The relation between man and nature is what was called the "point connecting humans and nature" in traditional Chinese philosophy.[28] The insight that reemerges full blown in Zhang Shiying's work is evident in this passage from one of Feng's later works,

> Humans are products of nature, but after they exist they also stand in opposition to nature. Facing them, first of all, is their opposition to nature. This is the opposition between the subjective and the objective. Their own thought, feelings, and intentions are the subjective, and nature is the objective. Although nature prepares all the conditions for life, such as sunlight and rainfall, they still must struggle with nature and change it, and only then can they sustain and improve their lives.[29]

He goes on to clinch the matter like this,

> As an individual, a natural scientist may possibly have faith in some kind of religion. However, as a scientist, he consciously or unconsciously accepts that the object of his investigation is an objective existence independent of the subjective.[30]

Other writers today build on Feng's insights. In generalizing about the history of Chinese thought, they have identified an obsession with harmonizing contradictions or dualities (inner-outer, self-others, old-new, heaven-humans) as a central characteristic of it.[31] They have included among the deficiencies of this approach the failure to separate the subjective and objective. Like the younger Feng, they note in this perspective a failure to distinguish the content of an idea about the world from its object in the world.

Concurrently, others have separated the technical terminology for regular laws or patterns of objective phenomena from those which pertain to the inner life of humans. This is in contrast to the traditional easy attribution of human ideas of purpose or rank to nature. This shift involves identifying "truth" as a term appropriate for talking about the laws of objective phenomena in the natural and social sciences, while relating "needs" clearly to subjective life. These writers hold that such terms should be used for their respective spheres. It is said that values have their source in needs, and should not therefore intrude into the search for truth or into the formulation of scientific theory. Here is how one author puts it:

> The true content of a theory does not include the knowing subject [perceiver] and does not change as a function of the subject. If we want to cause social science truly to reflect the essence and laws of social phenomena, we must ceaselessly strive to eliminate the aspect of the subject as transformer [of phenomena], we must eliminate the subject's needs and

> interests. And yet the critical evaluation of a theory is different. It reflects the relation of the needs of the knowing subject to the theory. Its content naturally cannot not include the subject. The necessary consistency of scientific principles applicable in a given case shifts as a function of the needs of the subject. The method of investigation in the social sciences can aid us to distinguish between what is a theory's true content and what is its critical evaluation, and decide under what circumstances critical evaluation impedes the truth of an investigation's results and must be completely avoided.[32]

The author of these words cites as a positive example the work of Ma Yinchu on China's population. Furthermore, as another writer argues, it is legitimate to make critical value judgments involving subjective social or political standards when we are talking about techniques, such as how a factory is built.[33] However, this is not the same as granting objective status to those values.

The marvelous thing about this development is that it explicitly picks out for criticism the crucial ingredients of that old demon, the fact-value fusion. This fusion persists in the work of legions of writers who have continued to read human subjectivity into the world of nature and still claim that human needs can and should inform our picture of the objective world. The unity of heaven and human lives on in their efforts. However, there is now not only dissent from the professional philosophers cited above, there is also growing level of dissent about traditional assumptions in popular culture as well.

A Popular Breakthrough

We can thank such professional theorists as Feng Youlan and Zhang Shiying for separating the realms of heaven and humans. As a result of their work, the traits discovered in the objective world and the scope of our knowledge about it can move beyond predictable limits. But why should we have any confidence that the opportunity provided by this theoretical breakthrough could have any wide-scale impact when the old ways of thinking still endure? One reason is that some Chinese outside the classroom or the theorist's study have begun to recognize that to act as though subjectively derived values have a privileged position in objective inquiry is dysfunctional.

One popular protest against narrowing the scope of inquiry appeared in a 1985 satire by Wang Meng, who was Minister of Culture during the Tiananmen riots of 1989. This story, "A Winter's Topic" ("Dongtian de huati") criticizes the tendency for scientific subject matter to be dealt with as merely an issue in the role relationships of the researchers.[34] Let me briefly summarize it here.

The central figure, Zhu Shendu, is a 63-year-old specialist in "physiological hygiene" (concerning the human body and sanitation) whose research field is "bathology" (*muyuxue*). His problem is this: in terms of the scientific standards of physiological hygiene, when and how should one bathe? Predictably, the satire begins with one of Zhu's partisans citing a model,

> Someone confirmed that the narrative in *The Great Learning* refers to the fact that bathing plus fasting is an aid to rectifying the mind, making the will sincere, self-cultivation, ordering the family, ruling the state, and bringing peace to the world.[35]

Zhu's own position is that (in terms of physiological standards) evening bathing is best. Enter a young graduate student researcher, returned from three years of study in Canada, who publishes a piece on Canadians that discusses their preference for morning baths. Others join in and the analysis quickly shifts from the facts of physiology and hygiene to moral and personal aspects of bathing practices. One critic of the returned student asks, "Why does he think that Canadian bathing methods are correct? ... Can it be that if Canadians are unfilial to their parents, we should be, too?"[36] The returned student is thus branded as unpatriotic for *describing* the Canadian approach. The critic then focuses on the young man's "disrespect" to the elder scientist manifest in his apparently disagreeing with him. The personal relation between the elderly bathologist and the young researcher becomes the issue, along with the political background of the debate. Wang Meng ends his satire with the plaintive questions, "Why do meaningful and meaningless debates all end by becoming debates about human relationships? . . . Why does this kind of debate force you to turn everything into something metaphysical and absolute?"[37]

I take hope in such irreverence. The fact that someone has called attention to the absurd aspect of making an objective matter into a debate about roles and relationships is encouraging. All the more so since such debates can have real and detrimental social consequences for the investigators. These are believable signs that alternative perspectives on the issues of concern in this study have penetrated to a certain depth among the general population.

However, in the end, controlling the intrusion of subjective values and undercutting the authority of models will not of themselves be sufficient to satisfy the conditions for objective inquiry. While there is nothing wrong with admitting that our needs and interests affect our hypotheses and theories about the world, from the Chinese position, this is tantamount to admitting unquestionable correspondence between the way things are and the way they should be. I believe we can and should go beyond social and personal assumptions in our attempts to formulate correctives. As I mentioned above, this would include legitimizing public criticism of hypotheses, evidence, and the inferences made from both. There are at least two conditions under which such criticism can flourish. There is some movement toward one and none toward the other.

The condition toward which some progress has been made is the elimination of theories stating that a certain group's perspective will be considered correct by virtue of its highly ranked "natural" or "historical" social station. This ascription of special access to the truth was equally the case with Confucian scholar-officials in pre-modern China and with Chinese Communist Party officials under the Maoist regime. In both instances, the superior group could always speak for what was the "true interest" of all other people. The shift away from this situation is evident in the following article, dating from 1987:

> The traditional way to differentiate social classes is not useful under present conditions. The new social relations, group relations, and interpersonal relations can no longer be classified in light of the owning of the means of production. Vocational, technical, and other sociological standards are becoming more and more useful. No single person or social organization or group can absolutely and completely represent and realize the interest of all people in society. The false impression of "no conflict" no longer exists. People's interests are no longer monolithic, but plural.[38]

This view goes along with the epistemological principle that different groups may perceive the same situation differently:

> An indisputable fact in China today is that there exist different interest groups whose understanding of the objective situation is different, and that the interest structure and distribution patterns are gradually being replaced by new rational ones.[39]

In spite of this healthy development, limitations on the criticism necessary to objective inquiry remain. That is, momentarily powerful political figures, from a village party secretary to a national leader, can impose their personal preferences and opinions on any process of inquiry. There are no trustworthy official channels for criticism that might dispute them, though it is now possible to submit criticisms to newspapers, and this a beginning. However, the creation of regular channels for public debate remains a serious challenge for China to tackle in the future.

In this study I have tried to illustrate how theoretical issues in the humanities (philosophy in particular) intersect with actual life experiences of people who themselves are not theoreticians. Unlike earlier historical periods, higher levels of education and better access to information—print and electronic—make participation in these debates possible for ordinary people. Ordinary people have always paid the price for living with the imperial Confucian style of inquiry. Now such people may also play a role in developing correctives to it.

In the end, my own sympathies lie with the approach of Feng Youlan, though not with the *li*[b] (principle-oriented) metaphysics on which he based it. I find no incompatibility between retaining the ideal of integrating knowledge and the retention of the subjective-objective distinction. We can try to control the intrusion of personal subjectivity or needs into the process of inquiry, while remaining cognizant that meaning grows as we increasingly understand relationships.

This is one of three positions in which I find the best of Chinese and Western philosophy to be mutually compatible. The other two emerge in the next chapter. One involves accepting Confucian models for purposes of self-cultivation, while remaining mindful of their harm to inquiry. The other is the retention of Confucian communitarian values in society while accepting the legitimacy of individual autonomy in inquiry.

CHAPTER FIVE

The Emergence of Autonomy as a Chinese Social Value

Individual autonomy can coexist with other, communitarian values in China. It also has an important role to play in scientific inquiry there. The writings of certain American philosophers of science have convinced me that this is the case, though they may not be specially concerned with China. In my Preface, I expressed gratitude to one of these philosophers, Peter Railton. What he and others enabled me to understand is that scientific inquiry is a social process, whose end product is usually a collective one. Further, individual autonomy need not be treated as an end in itself. In the context of inquiry, it can have instrumental worth, as a means or facilitator of good science. It does so by promoting the various hypotheses that a group of investigators concerned about a single problem may explore.

As I also stated in the Preface, I do not advocate unconventional behavior or rebellious beliefs as intrinsically good, nor do I advocate undermining China's traditional communitarian values and respect for authority, even if doing so were possible. Rather, I encourage the substitution of epistemic values consistent with the goals of scientific inquiry for the political and social values imposed on investigators by those with political power. In a previous chapter I referred to Jürgen Habermas' position that free and open communication and dissemination of information is one value consistent with scientific goals. This chapter adds autonomy as another.

I believe that when the value of individual autonomy has legitimacy, a multitude of individuals will feel free and motivated to put forth their own hypotheses when they study a problem. Autonomy, therefore, is a necessary condition for variability in theories. Where there is a variety of theories available in the process of inquiry, people learn from each other. Among various competing theories, some will prevail, due to the recognition in the scientific community of their explanatory strengths, breadth of application or problem-solving capability. This approach opposes single models and single authorities, such as those presented by political or community leaders. It does not oppose the authority of peers, however. Because the individual's particular prejudices may affect his theories, there is a place for the authority of peer evaluation and correction.

In the present chapter, I will outline the emergence of individual autonomy as a social value in Chinese theoretical and popular works. I believe these developments are necessary historical precursors for legitimizing individual autonomy as part of the social process of inquiry. I favor introducing autonomy as a legitimate value that, coexisting and competing with communitarian values, can play a powerful, positive role in the expansion of knowledge. As we have seen, breaking away from the imperial Confucian style of inquiry is a multifaceted affair. It includes a combination of theoretical breakthroughs, popular trends, and institutional changes. Below I will focus on the move away from reflexive reliance on models and will argue that this represents an opportunity for change. My contention is based on the striking convergence of interests in both elite theory and popular media around the single theme of autonomy. This suggests a significant historical development in the sense that the convergence of interest around autonomy has persisted since roughly 1980.

Although this chapter focuses on the shift away from following models in personal decision making, its message applies also to the kinds of technical decisions described in chapter 3. Needless to say, not everyone accepts this shift, and the emergence of autonomy as a value by no means signals the end of communitarian values. Indeed, the individual who makes a decision on his own authority or the team that does so on its authority alone may very well need community support to implement those decisions. Moreover, persons may favor autonomy in matters of career choice and scientific inquiry while prizing communitarian values or even the will of political authorities on matters of welfare and social stability. Social reality is rarely a simple matter.

But what kind of autonomy can present real challenges to the models imposed by authorities or set up in conventional beliefs? This question is intended to uncover a historical trajectory, and is not based on the belief that all such challenges are intrinsically worthwhile. My contention is that the idea of an autonomous self uncoupled from the belief that all clear-headed people think alike on general moral principles can play this role. In the following discussion, I will compare the evolution of such ideas in Europe with recent developments in China, identifying historical and philosophical sources for the emergence of an autonomy that is both uncoupled from a unitary moral perspective and also meets the needs of China's modern circumstances.

Elite Theory

The theory of autonomy and popular discourse about it in China have had an impact on each other. For example, both theoretical and popular realms by and large use the same vocabulary. Translators usually render the English word autonomy as *zizhu* (self-master) or *zizhi* (self-in-control). However, there are several other Chinese terms—*duli sikao* (independent thinking), *nengdongxing* (initiative), and, sometimes, *chuangzaoxing* (creativity)—that are frequently employed in theoretical and popular contexts where the English speaker would use "autonomy." Thus, there is really little precision in the use of these expressions.

Moreover, the meanings of almost all of these terms can be understood negatively or positively. From a negative standpoint, they refer to the absence of control over an individual person's actions or choices by an outside agent. That outside agent may be impersonal, such as a god, destiny, the traditional heavenly principle, or class and economic conditions in the Marxist sense. These terms may also refer to the absence of efforts by officials to use models or other means to enforce *datong* or *dayitong* (uniformity) of belief or work style. Positively speaking, these terms highlight the importance of individuals in creatively changing the world or their own life course.

An especially important term links theoretical discourse on autonomy and education theory. This is *zhutixing* (subjectivity), which takes its meaning from the centrality of the subject or actor as agent.[1] However, many theories about subjectivism have been sheparded into public discourse under the rubric of autonomy, because of their focus on the subject-as-agent. Since the late 1970s, subjectivism, a usage partially inspired by the work of Kant (1724–1804) and others has become the focus of theoretical discussions in which autonomy is the key issue. Subjectivity (as autonomy) means that the subject freely changes the world as a result of his choices. If we can visualize the two-millennia-long interest in *theories* of human nature as a premodern Confucian watersource, the twentieth century stream that flows from it has moved along three professional channels: philosophy, psychology, and literary theory. I will primarily discuss philosophy, but will also say a few words about the other fields because published accounts of autonomy theory appear across all three under the subjectivist umbrella. First, philosophy.

When the topic of subjectivity burst onto the philosophy scene in 1978, its focus was on the subject (the individual actor) helping to create something new in the world rather than being a passive recipient of stimuli.[2] Theorists envisioned it as the individual choosing or acting as an agent independent of the Party or official culture. Thus, subjectivity functioned as a temporary disguise for the topic of autonomy in philosophical and educational circles.

This point did not go unnoticed by Party intellectuals, who tried to forge versions of it more in keeping with the sources of Party orthodoxy. Thus, while some writers discussed subjectivity as choice, creativity, and the free development of the subject, many others borrowed the language of humanism from early Marx. These included the former *Peoples' Daily* editor Wang Ruoshui. Wang cited Marx on the goal of achieving "free-spirited individuality" through communism and his assertion that "the free development of each individual is a requirement for the free development of all people." Wang went on to advocate self-realization as man's highest need.[3] The question was, should the individual's choices be subject to Party interference? An answer in the affirmative was the clear position of the opposition, such as former secretary to Mao and honorary president of the Chinese Academy of Social Sciences, Hu Qiaomu (1912-1992). In his treatise opposing the advocates of self-realization, Hu stated that bourgeois humanism takes individualism as key, while socialist humanism values the people's democratic dictatorship.[4] He argued that the Party should retain primary authority.

Theoretical claims about the subject-as-agent hide two overlapping but essentially different ideas. One, which will not concern me here, is that the objective world is in some sense a construct; it is shaped by the subjective interests and interpretive paradigms of the individual agent.[5] The other meaning is psychological, and its implications are primarily ethical rather than epistemological: subjectivity is the ability and desirability of the individual to act autonomously. Where Mencius claimed that a compassionate, moral mind was essentially human, the subjectivists were equally unequivocal about subjectivity as a human trait: "Human subjectivity is the part of human nature which expresses man's essence in the most concentrated way; it is the quintessence of human nature."[6] These words make it clear that the topic of subjectivity fits easily into that central interest in Confucian philosophy, the theory of human nature. The traits assigned to it thereby attain elevated status. Guo Zhan, the author of those words, goes on to lay out what he regards those traits to be:

> Man only proves his own subjectivity when he has transformed the object [objective thing] through initiative, choice, and creativity, and self-consciously realizes human goals in the process of reifying the subject as it transforms the object. This gives full, free [rein to the] development of the subject itself.[7]

Like the expressive artist, the free person leaves the marks of his creativity on the things on which he acts. Chinese writers acknowledge that this theme has some European origins in the Kantian idea that man should be treated as an end and not as a means. To be considered as an end is to be self-controlled rather than directed by others.[8] But most of the German trappings, be they from Kant or the early Marx, faded into the background leaving the ideas of free initiative, choice, and creativity in the foreground. The strongest evidence for this is the appropriation of the issues of subjectivity to justify teaching these values in the schools. Examples of this will follow when I examine the popularization of autonomy. The intellectual position of aesthetician, Li Zehou, highlights the change in direction taken by the subjectivity movement in recent years. Although Li was one of the first to call attention to subjectivity when he discussed individual responsibility in a book on Kant, unlike Kant he had no particular interest in individual creativity or autonomy. Rather, the creativity of human groups collectively was his concern. The shift of the subjectivity movement to a focus on the individual self has left Li behind.[9]

A review of the meanings of subjectivity in China reveals that considerable inspiration from Wang Yangming has shaped modern ideas of autonomy. Wang encouraged individuals to turn to their innate moral sense in making decisions instead of relying on the authority of texts. If the emergence of autonomy undercuts the old style of inquiry, it will be, to that extent, a Chinese corrective. However, certain elements of today's notion of autonomy do not derive from Wang. One is the idea that individuals are the legitimate source of their own values, as those values motivate their actions. The perception of those values is no longer mediated by the innate content of a mind shared among all people, a common mind, as Wang Yangming taught. This development owes something to the ongoing exposure to Western ideas of individualism, which the Chinese access through, among other things, electronic media.

The other new element, developed in chapter 4, is the recent separation of the human from the heavenly realms, which is presently cast as the separation of the subjective from the objective. The separation of the subjective and the objective means that the two realms have important traits that are not shared. This enhances the autonomy of humans by freeing them from the constraints of so-called natural laws that are subject to official interpretation. The fascinating eventuality is that autonomy will be discussed in terms of the age-old Chinese paradigm: the unity of heaven and people. "Subjectivity" as a topic will evaporate, and autonomy will mean the *disunity* of heaven and humans. That is how the idea will be cast.

Chinese psychologists have noted the international movement away from Freudian biological reductionism and from behaviorism.[10] China's own interest in subjectivity places it in the international mainstream. Within the field of psychology, Lin Fang and others focus on such inner events as needs, potentialities, and motives. Though not using the term "subjectivism," they give such a central place to these inner events that it locates them squarely within this anti-behaviorist movement and within a departure from the economic determinism of conscious life prominent in their own recent Marxist history, which also downgraded the inner life of people.[11] In the process, a new value, self-realization, has made its way into social science, as the possibility of individual autonomy undercuts deterministic biological reductionism and behaviorism. Individual autonomy as a value is an aspect of self-realization. In this theory, individual autonomy is treated as a possibility (a factual matter) and as desirable (a value matter). The role of values in the study of motivation is accepted in this reassertion of the significance of the inner life. Widely, and across disciplines, values are anchored in claims about universal needs: "Value, i.e., a state of the object that is capable of satisfying certain needs of the subject, or the specific usefulness of the object for the subject…"[12] Self-realization is a basic need.[13] Because I myself prize individual autonomy, I praise Lin Fang for this point.

Finally, autonomy, initiative, and creativity also constitute the core of theoretical discussions of standards in literature when the literary specialists write on subjectivity. They say things such as this: In creating literature, the author should treat persons as those who "act and think according to their own mode," and the writer should give a character the right to act freely and independently, "having self-worth based in consciousness of autonomy."[14]

It is critical to remember that the subjectivity movement in China had a local origin and was not simply an offshoot of the imported doctrine of German Kantianism.[15] The immediate catalyst for the emergence of the subjectivity theme was Deng Xiaoping's resurrection of the Maoist slogan "seek truth from facts"[16] to which Deng added "… and make practice the sole criterion of truth." In Marxist-Maoist epistemology, a person gains access to facts by engaging in practice, a technical term in Marxism meaning interacting with the objective world. Before 1978, the term introduced a bit of activism—learn by participating in revolutionary practice—into the process of knowing, in contrast to Lenin's theory of reflection, which had cast knowing in a passive light with the mind as a reflecting mirror. After 1978, the idea of practice developed new meanings. It raised the issue of how much the individual subjectively contributes to an interaction. "Practice" became a way of talking about "subjectivity" in an epistemological sense (*zhuguanxing*) in contrast to subjectivity as autonomy. The subjectivity movement is an unequivocal and radical departure from the Leninist theory of reflection that along with Maoism dominated epistemology in China from 1949 to 1976.

Autonomy in Popular Life

"Popular media" is an elusive expression. What are the popular media in China and whose voice is raised in them? One possible answer is that there cannot possibly be anything popular about work that is openly published because the government controls almost all print organs. This position assumes centralized state control of whatever appears.

There is another, more compelling approach, however. It rejects the assumption that the state or leaders can either produce or be mindful of everything that appears, even in state-controlled organs. It assumes that the real people who edit and write have a variety of perspectives. Even though they work for governmental organizations, there is no reason they cannot be considered part of the popular media. They may self-censor or they may have unmanifest thoughts that only a skilled survey researcher could access. But even within the limits of self-censorship, variety exists. *Zhongguo qingnian* (*China Youth*) is the classic case of a journal that belongs to a powerful state agency, the Central Committee of the Communist Youth League. Yet a variety of opinions can be found in its pages. The leaders of China are, after all, a group of busy people who surely do not intervene every time an editor of a newspaper or journal or publishing house decides to publish or promote a certain theme. Additionally, there are many different types of editors and reporters. If there is a government mouthpiece with anything like a single point of view, it is the *New China News Agency*.

My conclusion is that the sources to which I will refer are popular in the sense that they contain expressions of mainstream citizen viewpoints. This does not mean that these are the only mainstream views or even that they are the only views their various authors hold. But they are surely views in addition to, and different in social origin from, those in scholarly journals. In any case, views in the press do not typically originate in the heads of the senior leadership.[18] Given the broad scope and readership of what I treat as the popular media, there is an objective basis for underscoring the historical significance of the emergence of the topic of autonomy.

Autonomy has entered the mainstream of urban popular youth culture as part of the rediscovery of the self. Some of the most compelling evidence for this can be found in a series of articles in the journal *China Youth* in 1980[19] and two overview studies in the same journal, one in 1988[20] and another in 1992, that summed up developments of the previous years on this topic. The 1992 article makes the point that a new era in the study of the self has arrived with the popularization of ideas that had been in circulation since 1980. "Seven or eight years ago 'the self', to a very significant degree, was an abstract 'theory'...", centering on such ideas as self-design, self-realization, independence, and knowing the self. However, now, the author continues, "'the theory' has already become conventional wisdom." It is simply assumed that individuals should choose their own future course (*xuanze ziji de qiantu*)[21] One of its central slogans is "Do what *you yourself* want to do" (*gan ziji xiang gan de shi*). The convention now includes the belief that, "My choice may not be approved by everyone, but I believe that it is the most valuable."[22] Often, the choice in question is about life plan or career. It would be difficult for a central government to return to fostering one-minded uniformity in a populace that has taken such "conventional wisdom" to heart.

This development, the new centrality in popular culture—especially youth culture—accorded to terms around the idea of self has coexisted with a certain degree of government oppression where expressions of autonomy are manifest in dissident opinions or lifestyles. The government has allowed choice in consumption and spare time activities. The rediscovery of the self has coexisted with an official attempt to impose uniform collectivist values that are usually equated with patriotism. To obey the Party is to be patriotic, because the leaders always know what is in the interest of all the Chinese people. The emergence of autonomy is in fact a parallel thread in the culture, although it is often ignored by observers. Instead reporters generally favor noting the cynicism bred by government attempts at creating uniformity.

The gradual popularization of autonomy as a value has occurred in concert with condemnation of the reflexive emulation of models. Articles in *China Youth* have often paired the praise of autonomy with a critique of reliance on models and the uniformity that can come with it. For example, the reader is warned not to copy the PLA hero Lei Feng because he accepted whatever the leaders said as right.[23] The earliest writings in the movement carry titles such as, "How People in Our Society Have Been 'Standardized' [*moshihua*]."[24] "People are all possessed of selves and there cannot be a kind of superior person who forgets himself," says one writer.[25] Of course, those who emulate models are supposed to forget themselves in the process.

The authors of these critiques are aware of the philosophical assumptions that permit this kind of loss of individuality. For example, one paean to the sacredness of the self says, "During the last few decades, one needed only to bring up the topic of 'person' and inevitably the first thing to be considered was the [social] whole, only after this could the individual be addressed. It was as though the individual is first part of a collective and only secondarily an individual."[26]

Summing up developments seven or eight years later, someone wrote that "in those previous periods, the youth had only one ideal: to be a worker, peasant, or soldier." He continued that there was something about that fact that supressed creativity in most people.[27] People differ in endowment and in the types of contribution they can make to their country, which makes the ideal of uniformity impractical. Concrete reactions against this self-destroying uniformity have taken many popular forms.

That some 60,000 young people dared to express their belief in the individual's independent worth in print in the spring of 1980 is itself testimony to autonomy's popularization. Factory workers, farmers, commercial people, students and soldiers all wrote to the editors of *China Youth*.[28] In the 1988 retrospective that reprinted their letters, their writings are full of phrases such as *zizun* (self-respect), *zi'ai* (self-love), *zili* (establishing the self), *zixin* (self-confidence) and *ziwo jiazhi* (self-worth). Their central interest was autonomy, with special attention to assuming control over their lives: "Young people want to create and control their own destinies; this is the exercise of man's basic power."[29]

Lest one think that this movement was only an urban phenomenon, the ten-year retrospective documents a prominent rural manifestation. This was a significant change in marriage practices, namely, the increased frequency of elopement. Eloping meant a defacto choice of partner made by the youths themselves, a practice not accepted by adults.[30]

The language with which ordinary people discussed the emergence of very modest choices in elections is also revealing. This can be seen with the introduction of the "Varied Quota Elections" system (*cha'e xuanzhu*) in 1982, in which choices rested on the fact that there were more candidates than posts. Many early elections of this type were held in municipal districts. Universities, as part of those districts, helped them vote against the candidates recommended by the Party. A few years later, people in provincial legislatures voted against Party candidates for governor. Journalists spoke of the new-style elections as "demonstrating the individual's own right and value." And they also cited ordinary people using this kind of language: "We prefer the method of "competing horses" (*saima*) to decide which horse can go one thousand *li* in a day, to that of "[leaders] looking over the horses" (*xiangma*), where officials pick the winners." Some people went so far as to say that the former approach manifests the worth of "the individual's own opinion."[31]

Prize-winning novellas of the 1980s reveal the same sentiment. Characters no longer needed to represent a typical Party or official class model; rather, they could demonstrate their independence. In "Eyes with Tears" a rightist escapes from the farm where he did years of forced labor. The letter he leaves behind reveals his principles: "First, I will not betray my country—because I have been nurtured on oriental milk; second, I will not steal—because I regard that as shameless conduct. I want to rely on my own two hands to open a future path for my life."[32] In "The Emperor at the Corner of the Market" are these lines:

> One day, Wu Yue determined to choose being in private business as his profession. He disliked being manipulated by other people, and he wanted to take charge of his work time himself. He wanted to test his strengths, to live just like a contemporary foreigner—when busy to be as busy as a prisoner in forced labor, and when at play to be as leisurely as a genuine playboy.[33]

The educational system is the most visible popular platform for the value of autonomy in the post-Mao period; it permeates professional publications that describe educational guidelines and practices. In addition, it is among the most reliable guarantees that an alternative to the old style of inquiry will endure.

The vocabulary of the subjectivity movement has moved into pedagogy, but it continues to be window dressing. The real issue is advocacy for the value of autonomy in education. For example, an article entitled "On the Development of Human Subjectivity and the Establishment of the Principle of Modern Educational Subjectivity" appeared in one of the premier educational journals in 1989. It links together the cluster of ideas that I have placed under the autonomy umbrella: "This basic human essence [subjectivity] includes initiative [*nengdongxing*], autonomy *[zizhuxing]*, and creativity [*chuangzaoxing*]." Individual particularity (*teshu*) also has a place in the concept.[34]

The ultimate justification for teaching this value takes us to the first two principles of ethics. Throughout the Maoist period, the perfected person was described in educational and other circles as manifesting "all-round development" (*quanmian fazhan*). Its precise content changed with the ideology of the moment. In the late 1950s, Great Leap, and early Cultural Revolution years, it referred to the ability to do both manual and desk labor, with some degree of experience in and willingness to do both. At other times it came close to the European Renaissance ideal, the Leonardo model. With the advent of the subjectivity movement, the fully developed student was one whose subjectivity had been cultivated to bolster the intellectual faculties, for instance, the ability to understand and contribute to science.[35]

The other basic ethical principle is needs, the root of value. We learn that the task of education is to satisfy peoples'*need* to fully realize their individual potential. The individual's life has the components of knowledge, physical strength, and moral judgment, which are particular to each discreet person.[36] Subjectivity education can satisfy the need to fully develop these. What the advocates of subjectivity education hope the schools will accomplish can be brought into sharper focus against the backdrop of what they oppose.

An important pedagogical work that appeared in the decade after Mao's death contains a study entitled, "Cultivating Socialist China's Masters of the Twenty-first Century" (*Peiyang ershiyi shiji shehui zhuyi Zhongguo de zhuren*). It is subtitled: "The results of educational experiments concerning elementary students' all-round development, from September 1983 to August 1985."[37] Here, professional educators engaged in a genuine experimental method, challenging the old rule that "the student must accept what the teacher says." The authors note that the new age requires students to possess "the scientific spirit... independence of thought and courage in pursuing creative ends." By way of application, the article advised that students in literature classes should not be prompted with the viewpoints of a single authority; they should not have to share the same interpretation as members of a group. Diversity of thought is an important formative component in creative thinking. The operative words are *dute* (uniqueness), *biantong* (flexibility), and *dulisikao* (independence of thought).[38] Autonomous activity (*zizhu huodong*) describes the kind of behavior to be cultivated.[39]

If a condition in which one is forced into intellectual conformity is the enemy, alternatives can be clearly laid out. First, the student has the right to put forth his own ideal and goals, and select and accept or reject the content of what is taught.[40] Only in this way, with the student having the power of self-conscious choice, can one speak of subjectivity in education. Using the language of self-cultivation (*ziwo xiuyang*), the guides tell the reader that students should develop self-consciousness by comparing themselves with others, practice self-evaluation, know their own thoughts, feelings, and good and bad points.[41] Self-education involves "the ability to play a role in self-design, deciding to establish an ideal image for the self; to be self-directed in the selection of a value orientation; these are all natural and are rights of the individual."[42] Teachers should take note of each student's individual characteristics in teaching.[43]

In the end, the outside analyst must be cautious about how different educators will interpret these themes. There will surely be those who limit the scope of autonomy to self-motivation in study habits. This is a far cry from the position of other advocates of subjectivity who see it as a principle for moral and intellectual growth, providing an opportunity for individuals to successfully grapple with life's central questions.

John Dewey and his disciples introduced many of these themes to China back in the 1920s, and advocates at the end of the century acknowledge a partial debt to Dewey. But now their positions are reinforced by other movements in popular culture, by China's entrepreneurial age, and by international educators with whom China's leaders in the field have contact. Thus, there is some expectation that their positive impact will endure. It is possible that the reflexive reliance on antecedent models still taught in many Chinese schools may diminish.

I will conclude by shifting from ideas discussed in the popular media to an account of actual behavior illustrating the conflict that has arisen between advocates on both sides of the model issue. During the late 1980s, the government set up two young people as "model citizens." Their duty was to travel across the country extolling the virtues of collectivism, patriotism, and the Party. At one point, they and a third "model citizen" had a feisty exchange with some youths in the special economic zone of Shenzhen. One youth impolitely concluded the meeting by saying, "I don't think that there is any market in Shenzhen for your ideas." A Shenzhen journalist's account of the exchange refers to an article written by one of the youths who had confronted the models, entitled, "Culture of the gods" ("Shen de wenhua"). The journalist's report makes the following points,

> The models propagated by the Chinese [government] for thirty years have all been gods, whereas the urgent need is for a human culture. He [the youth] believes that Li Yanjie and Qiu Xiao [two of the models], in coming to lecture, make announcements, and spread propaganda, still constitute a kind of 'culture of the gods,' or 'culture of models.' They take a certain kind of model and try to make it appeal to all people, [or advocate] one kind of conduct and one kind of idea to make everyone the same. The result is to take the living, individuated 'many' and make them into a uniform 'one.'[44]

This incident caused an uproar in Beijing. In the end, I place considerable hope in what is happening in the popular youth culture.

The significant thing about this example is that it recognizes the forced and unnatural uniformity of mind that was the ultimate purpose of training people to rely on models. The utility of educators' employing models of a specific skill or virtue is never in question. Indeed, it is a real strength of the Chinese model emulation practices. However, what this youth discovered is that models who stand for the possibility and desirability of uniform thought and conduct occupy a ghost world that is different from the real world. The real world is one of endless particularity and we should never expect to come to the end of its variety. It cannot be made uniform for any length of time. This is the real, objective world that inquiry in China may now be primed to discover.

The most promising opportunity for an alternative to copying models, then, lies in the new emergence and positive endorsement of the value of individual autonomy in China. Armed with confidence in his possession of the ability to make independent decisions and of the legitimacy of so doing, the individual may be likely to trust his own judgment or permit others to trust theirs, rather than to look to a model. This, at any rate, is my hypothesis.

Two Paths to Autonomy

The Historical Path

Western ideas about nature have not been immune from the kinds of beliefs that have distorted inquiry and are part of the imperial style in China. Therefore, there is no claim of cultural superiority in my argument. However, there are historical factors that facilitated the movement away from those ideas in the West, and knowledge of them can prepare us to better understand and assess the opportunities for change that now exist in China. It will help us to realize that there are objective reasons for both traditional premises about knowledge and for their replacements, and that we can foster the conditions leading to those replacements.

As important as distinguishing the subjective and objective realms is, as important as the stance of Feng Youlan was, there is a limit to the degree of separation that any investigator can attain. In the West, no one except a survivor of the nearly extinct positivist doctrines would take the position that the investigator's needs and values can be totally eliminated from inquiry. The positivist philosophers of the 1930s and later claimed that science can be entirely value free.[45] As I indicated in chapter 1, most who study inquiry in the social and natural sciences today take a very different stance. They assume that science has its own values. The criteria that determine which data are relevant rest on theories that may reflect social influences. The point is to try to make sure that only those values that are consistent with the mission of scientific inquiry prevail in inquiry, and to establish controls for the social influences. This means guarding against the intrusion of other social and political values into the process. The investigators must be protected from those who claim to be the ultimate source of truths or who establish models of such truths that must be followed. Galileo was mindful of this when he wrote:

> And that to want other people to deny their own senses and to prefer to them the judgment of others, and to allow people utterly ignorant of a science or an art to become judges over intelligent men and to have power to turn them round at their will by virtue of the authority granted to them; these are the novelties with power to ruin republics and overthrow states.[46]

Helen Longino argues that most inquiry is social, that is, involving many people. The personal and cultural values of participants, then, cannot be kept entirely separate from the theories the investigators use to explain phenomena. Among other examples, she points to the theory of sexual division of labor (men hunt; women gather or nurture) as colored by social values that infect inquiry in even the most recent evolutionary studies and in neuroendocrinology.[47]

It is also certainly the case that, regarding events with political implications, Western decision makers have been guided by models selected for reasons other than their fit with the situation under investigation. Richard E. Neustadt and Ernest R. May have written an entire book, *Thinking in Time: The Uses of History for Decision Makers* about the successful and unsuccessful models our modern decision makers have copied.[48] Social values that have nothing to do with good inquiry continue to show up in our science and in our political investigations.

However, if the process of inquiry is social, so are the protections from abuse. They center on equality of intellectual authority. That authority must be shared and not located in a single source. There cannot be a single official model. Thus, hypotheses must be available for testing by anyone with the necessary education. Peer review opens the door to regularized evaluation of theories.[49] Open criticism is key.

Historical conditions arose in the West that permitted scientists like Galileo to challenge—eventually with success—the intrusion of theological and political authorities into matters of inquiry. There were several historical developments that may have contributed to the shift away from a ready acceptance of beliefs imposed by one authority or another. James Q. Wilson names two candidates. One was the rise of consensual marriage, affirmed by Pope Alexander III in the twelfth century. The Pope rejected the claims of parental consent, and decreed that a marriage in which consent was freely acknowledged by a woman and a man of the appropriate ages was valid. This diminished clan and parental control over an important decision.[50] Another development cited by Wilson emerged in England in the thirteenth century. This was the establishment of laws that reccognized privately-held, rather than collectively owned, land. The control of clans over individuals again diminished as individuals gained the ability to purchase and to sell land, or to own private property.[51]

My own candidate among the contributors to change in the West has no counterpart in China. This was the existence in sixteenth and seventeenth century Europe of religious congregations that had no chance of achieving dominance within a state. Churches that had official state support commonly became intolerant toward other denominations. Citizens belonging to the smaller religious groups responded by demanding toleration of their beliefs by the state. John Plamenatz has identified as chief players in this movement the Socinians, who became known as Unitarians in Transylvania, and the Anabaptists and Baptists. The Socinians affirmed that every person must be permitted to determine by himself which parts of the New Testament are accessible to reason and which are matters of faith. The Calvinists and Lutherans obviously were also players, though the Socinians went much farther by accepting the principle of diversity of opinion. The 1574 Socinian *Confession of Faith* specifically criticized attacks on dissidents.[52] Eventually in the West the momentum that began in religious congregations for freedom of *religious* belief evolved into political and philosophical arguments for freedom of belief on all matters.[53] This is clearly the case with John Locke's famous *Letter Concerning Toleration*. Western openness to the criticism of opinions and hypotheses has its roots, among other places, in the social and intellectual developments that sprang from these congregations' positions on freedom of religious belief.

Pointing to the historical role of religious dissidence in helping to form the Western idea of autonomy does not permit the inference that diversity of religious or other belief is *in itself* desirable, with no concern for shared beliefs. Thomas Hobbes is a good example of someone directly familiar with religious squabbles in seventeenth-century England. As Edwin Curley has pointed out, Hobbes was mindful of how religious dissent prevented rather than facilitated stable government, and that civil society was a necessity, lest people tear their own communities apart.[54] I would add that civil society requires shared values: toleration of different beliefs, toleration of a non-governmental sector, respect for the authority of elected officials, and respect for the laws by which those officials exercise their will and for the laws that protect people against their rulers.

Mindful of this observation, I can return to the issue of the historical role of religious dissent in the emergence of autonomy. In China, imperial Confucianism treated the emperor as the intermediary between heaven and humans. All humans and their organizations were subordinate to the emperor who sought a condition of "one-mindedness" throughout the realm. The monk Huiyuan (334–417) argued that monks are subject to monastic law and not to secular rules and should not have to bow down before a king. But that view did not prevail. The state exerted its control over the clergy (excepting self-appointed village priests) through official monitoring of ordination, begun in 747, but not widely enforced until the eleventh century. This included an examination system for entry into the monastic life modeled on the civil service examinations. A periodic census of monks was initiated in 729 that gave the state a register of monks, an additional tool of control. The highest-level supervision of all monks was a civil official, not a cleric. The state also controlled which temples had official authorization. There was no direct line from the individual to heaven, the Buddha, or Laozi that could circumvent the emperor as the state, the ultimate arbiter of acceptable beliefs on all matters.

This is not to say that religious congregations (*hui*) with heterodox beliefs did not exist and operate apart from the state. There were social congregations at the village level that occasionally had these traits. On a larger scale, there were groups such as the White Lotus Society, which often operated in secret, their members worshipping their own deities who were not officially sanctioned. From time to time these communities were viewed as a threat by the state, which never gave up its ideology of the emperor as ultimate standard and model for all minds.

Even nonreligious organizations in late imperial times, such as merchant guilds, operated successfully only with official patronage.[55] During the Communist period, groups from chess players' associations to trade associations to journalists' associations have had to maintain relations with official agencies in order to function; they are still called "affiliated units" (*guagou danwei*). The ideal of one-mindedness has endured, with the state as the ultimate standard of truth. The idea of permissible dissidence, of toleration of variety in beliefs, of open criticism of theories, can never flourish under these circumstances. We have seen that one of the major instruments used by the state to enforce this one-mindedness has been the establishment of models. Because models generally have official status, the solutions they dictate are not open to public examination and criticism.

The recent emergence of nongovernmental organizations (NGOs) in China represents a crucial development toward the toleration of plurality of beliefs such as the religious congregations in Europe helped to foster. While some of the NGOs have roots that go back to the 1930s, there was a real burgeoning of their numbers in the 1980s. Although many of these groups are simple hobby clubs, all were forced, at least nominally, to re-establish ties with government agencies after June, 1989.[56]

Even more important than the NGOs themselves is the existence of laws that protect people against their rulers and that permit organizations to be independent of, rather than dependent on, government agencies. Such laws protect expressions of momentarily unpopular opinions or those that run contrary to official positions. Thus, the existence of such laws and respect for them rounds out the conditions for the exercise of individual choice.

With China having no legacy of religious congregations struggling for the principle of freedom of belief, the historical question arises as to why conditions in China now provide opportunities for discourse about individual autonomy. I would suggest that the emergence of individual and local entrepreneurial agents in the free market economy is key. Such an explanation would apply also to the 1930s, a period to which I have traced other roots of this paradigm shift. I have already given examples from popular literature of the convergence of the themes of autonomy and the private entrepreneur. Entrepreneurs prize the right to decide which beliefs motivate their lives and affect their balance sheets. The free market in newsprint has been another avenue for the promotion of autonomy and it has grown rapidly, selling popular publications in which *self*-gratification (sexual and other) appears as a persistent theme.[57]

The Philosophical Path

Many thoughtful Americans will probably tell you if asked that autonomy is the core trait of human beings. It has the same stature in our culture as the sense of benevolence or compassion did in Confucian culture ever since the elevation of the teachings of Mencius.

Our idea of autonomy has its roots in the doctrine of free choice or free will. This idea in turn has several sources. When clustered with the idea of individual responsibility, it served as one of the means for absolving an omnipotent and good God of blame for evil in the world. The source of human evil is the abuse of free will by persons. Augustine in the early years and Descartes in the modern period presented this position most forcefully. This religious context is missing from Confucian discussions of choice making. Further, Confucians make an important place for literal thoughtlessness or the absence of choice making. The sage is morally spontaneous. He reflexively does the right thing, acting in a manner that is appropriate to the external situation. The Western idea of autonomy is inconceivable apart from choice making: a person's actions are the result of his own choices rather than another person's coercive acts or threats.

Autonomy is also one of the core values making up the Western ethics of individualism. As a popular, unsystematic creed, individualism doubtless owes something to the concerns of commercial and agricultural entrepreneurs in modern England and America.

Our modern Western idea of autonomy received its most influential formulation by Kant in the eighteenth century. But Arthur Danto has noted something important that will be clear to any reader of the *Foundations of the Metaphysics of Morals*: "The rational being is perceived as legislator, but then each legislator or rational being enacts only those principles each other legislator would enact upon suitable ratiocination, so that in the end everyone must think alike."[58] Danto was referring to decisions about general moral principles rather than nuanced choices that take into account the specific details of a situation.

According to Kant, every rational person should act only on maxims that specify duties that everyone should carry out, or whose effects are universally desirable. There is uniformity in the duties that people might derive from this categorical imperative. He lists these examples: Rejecting suicide, desisting from false promises that one knows he cannot fulfill, developing one's talents, and helping someone in need.[59] There is no idiosyncrasy here. Any rational person will discover these to be duties. In addition, any rational being is committed to treating other such beings as ends in themselves and not as means. Morality is possible only when people recognize what he calls "common laws."[60]

I argue that so long as autonomy is paired with this idea that all people who think correctly will think alike, the philosophical door is open to authorities who can undercut the force of autonomy. This is because some people will claim that others do not think rationally or clearly. Therefore, those who do think clearly can legitimately think for the others, since, if rational, they would come to the same conclusion. This was certainly the case with Kant. In his essay, "What is Enlightenment," Kant defended the necessity of tutelage for the unenlightened. He wrote that many people bring on themselves paternalistic supervision through the lack of will to use their inborn reason.

> Enlightenment is man's release from his self-incurred tutelage. Tutelage is man's inability to make use of his understanding without direction from another. Self-incurred is this tutelage when its cause lies not in lack of reason but in lack of resolution and courage to use it without direction from another.[61]

We now live in an age of enlightenment, since Kant believed that most people in his time were still learning to think for themselves. Most people needed fetters, leashes, or constraints to guide and circumscribe their values and actions. Thus, in Kant's day an enlightened monarchy was better for tutoring people than a republic whose success would depend on their ready decision-making skills.[62]

Within the philosophical trajectory in Europe, the beginning of a break with the combination of autonomy and same-thinking emerged with the German Romantics in the first few decades of the nineteenth century. Friedrich Schleiermacher (1768–1834) rebelled against the Kantian idea that there is universal reason to which all people conform. Instead, he said that each person combines the attributes of being human in a unique way. A study on another Romantic writer of the era, Friedrich von Schlegel (1772–1829), describes Schegel's take on uniqueness this way:

> In the fullness of individual differences Schlegel sees a new moral law ... For him every infinite individual is God. For "it is just individuality that is the original and eternal in man: mere personality is not so momentous. To pursue the cultivation and development of this individuality as one's highest calling would be divine egoism."[63]

The source of uniqueness is *innerlichkeit,* meaning to be inner, to turn to inner resources and away from conformity to popular culture. It is like Thoreau's notion of a man not keeping pace with his companions because he hears "a different drummer."

Needless to say, some of the Romantics, such as Goethe, combined the glorification of uniqueness with a belief in the individual artist's ability to express a universal truth.[64] But, as Steven Lukes has shown, the idea of valuing the *different* drummer crossed the English channel and had an enormous impact on Anglo-American thought and political action. The bridge was the Romantic Wilhelm von Humboldt, who J.S. Mill explicitly credits in *On Liberty*. With this document of Mill's as a watershed, the philosophical conditions for a new vision of autonomy were complete. Freedom of choice coexisted with the ideal of "genius, and the necessity of allowing it to unfold freely both in thought and in practice...."[65] Here was a complete break with from Kant's "necessary leashes."

Kant is not a strict parallel for China's Wang Yangming, because, among other reasons, he rejected intuitionism. But in the evolution of the idea of autonomy, they share crucial stances: that the individual was the ultimate authority on general moral rules, and that clear-headed people all think alike.

Making the point that moral knowledge is universal, Wang wrote that,

> In innate knowledge and innate ability, men and women of simple intelligence and the sage are equal. Their difference lies in the fact that the sage alone can extend [act on] his innate knowledge....[66]

Because we possess this capability, hypothetically we do not need to consult texts as authorities.[67] Thus, the individual is reckoned the ultimate authority. But the content of these ultimate authorities is the same because the mind that people share is the same; it does not possess individual and innate differences.[68] Its content, as perceived by the individual, includes universal familial feelings and loyalty.[69]

As with Kant, the combination of individual autonomy and same-thinking opens the philosophical door to tutelage. Wang tells us that ordinary people's minds are clouded by selfish desires.[70] In his political writings on the Community Compact that he helped promote in southern Jiangsi in 1518, he favored methods that enforce sameness in thought and deed (one-mindedness) through peer pressure orchestrated by the authorities in the name of moral instruction.

As I explained in chapter 1, the important early twentieth century figures, Sun Yat-sen and Chiang Kai-shek were both disciples of Wang Yangming. They perpetuated his belief in both autonomy and the idea that clear-headed people think the same. And they enforced a system of tutelage, as Sun called it, during that period because they held that people could not properly think for themselves. The leadership of the Kuomintang were the teachers, and the Ministry of Education was their instrument.

A change began to emerge in the late 1970s with the subjectivity movement and popular developments that introduced a degree of tolerance for individualistic pluralism. However, this is by no means widely accepted in China and has not replaced the communitarian values for which Chinese society is well-known. But it does enjoy a following at the elite and popular levels. On at least some important issues, the individual has become the authority, and clear-thinking people may think differently, rejecting models and uniformity in the process. The paradigm has begun to shift from Wang Yangming, just as it shifted from Kant in the West on the issue of uniformity among rational thinkers.

Conclusion

There have been many competing ideologies in the post-Mao era and the movement that I have described is just one of them. A principal change in China is the new legitimacy of autonomy, if only in certain restricted spheres at the popular level. But an open door is an open door. The opportunities available with this partial shift from models to the individual are considerable in the area of problem solving.

While stressing the damage that the old imperial style has wrought in inquiry into social problems, I conclude by applauding with equal vigor the benefits that it can bring in the way of self-discipline, self-development, and community order. This cluster of beliefs endures in China because, in spite of its damage in the arena of inquiry, in other ways it works. People do effectively learn to do the right thing by emulating models. We call them role models, and psychologists call the process observational learning. To be single-minded in commitment to a value is a form of willpower that can give the individual an edge. Those who practice the martial arts know that concentrating on one thing and avoiding distractions focuses the energy needed to succeed. Discipline involves mindfulness of and acceptance of a standard. When there is a convergence of what a person has to do and of what he believes is right, there can be spontaneity in moral action. Although spontaneity is rarely a virtue in inquiry, it may very well be a virtue in routine ethical behavior. With such spontaneity there is less likelihood of the cynicism or self-deceit that can distract from doing the right thing. Finally, while it is true that a belief in the legitimacy of individual judgment, unfettered by political or social constraints, is essential to successful inquiry, there are also advantages to its competitor, the collectivist ideal. Those advantages are directly realized in community order. Reliability or predictability in relational groups and the predictability of action on the part of members contribute to social order, reducing one source of anxiety in people affected by such actions.

So I end by saying that in evaluating Chinese theories and practices concerning knowledge, its is essential to distinguish between premises as they apply to inquiry and to what the Confucians have called for so many centuries self-cultivation. Some of the premises with which this book has been concerned may be clarified and reformulated bearing in mind the distinction between inquiry and self-cultivation. For example, models of complex organizations, situations, or policies that contain detailed recipes for an investigator to follow (such as that of the Daqing oil fields) stand a good chance of not being useful in the search for solutions to problems. There is too much room for slippage between the structure of the model and the circumstances under study. Models that exemplify concretely simple charater traits or attitudes are often effective in transforming social behavior. This is especially the case if individuals wish to change, as do those receptive to Confucian teachings on self-cultivation. Models, moral spontaneity, and concern for group judgment have played a positive role in nurturing the steadfast Confucian heros who inspire many Chinese.

I advocate the replacement of the reflexive reliance on models in inquiry with individual autonomy and the other epistemological approaches I have championed in this study. In proper measure, these are compatible with the maintenance of model-driven forms of character training that endure from the past. Indeed, I believe there to be room enough for both individual judgment and collectivist values in the robust society of modern China.

Notes

Notes to Preface

1. Philip Kitcher, *The Advancement of Science* (New York: Oxford University Press, 1993).

2. Kitcher, 303. This work was brought to my attention by my colleague Peter Railton, Department of Philosophy, University of Michigan. Railton helped clarify the issues for me. An earlier work that also deals with the social nature of inquiry is Helen E. Longino, *Science as Social Knowledge* (Princeton: Princeton University Press, 1990).

3. Kitcher, 388.

4. Some of Mao's own writings on cognition and contradictions would be an exception, but he mixes up dialectical principles ultimately derived from historical materialism with principles based on the guerrilla experience, as I will show.

I refer the reader interested in the hard sciences and in natural dialectics to H. Lyman Miller's *Science and Dissent in Post-Mao China: The Politics of Knowledge* (Seattle: University of Washington Press, 1996). It identifies the contributions of certain scientists in the 1980s to the debate on the political autonomy of the scientific investigator. Fang Lizhi, an astrophysicist and democracy advocate, made a speech in Shanghai in 1986 in which he said, :"[State] documents pertaining to cultural developments, especially science, no longer invoke Marxism.... Marxism's authority in scientific circles was flawed from the beginning because true science cannot be guided by any rigid dogma." See Fang Lizhi, "Democracy, Reform, and Modernization," in *China Spring* 1.2, (March–April 1987): 17.

Notes to Chapter One

1. For a highly readable, fictionalized account of these matters, see Alice Tisdale Hobart, *Oil for the Lamps of China* (New York: Bantam Books, 1945), especially 136–137, 327–328. This book is based on the direct experience of Ms. Hobart and her husband, who together spent many years with Standard Oil in China. In 1960 I had many hours of conversation with her closest friend about those years.

2. Donald J. Munro, "The Chinese View of Alienation," *China Quarterly* 59, (July–September 1974): 580–82.

3. Francis M. Cornford, *Plato's Timaeus* (New York: Library of Liberal arts, 1959), 20, [30a].

4. Len Doyal and Roger Harris, *Empiricism, Explanation, and Rationality* (London: Routledge and Kegan Paul, 1986), 30–31.

5. Stephen Jay Gould, *Hen's Teeth and Horses Toes* (New York: W.W. Norton, 1983), 40–41.

6. A.C. Crombie, *Science, Optics, and Music in Medieval and Early Modern Thought*, (London: Hambledon Press, 1990), 356.

7. From Morris R. Cohen and Ernest Nagel, *An Introduction to Logic and Scientific Method* (New York: Harcourt Brace Jovanovich, 1934), reprinted as "Scientific Method" in Melvin Rader, *The Enduring Questions* (New York: Holt Rinehart and Winston, 1980), 322.

8. Ibid., 323.

9. Chad Hansen, "Individualism in Chinese Thought," in Munro, *Individualism and Holism: Studies in Confucian and Taoist* Values (Ann Arbor: Center for Chinese Studies, The University of Michigan, 1985), 51.

10. D.C. Lau, trans., *Mencius* (Middlesex, England: Penguin, 1970) VIIA.1, 182.

11. Ibid., IA.5, 53.

12. Burton Watson, trans., *Hsün Tzu: Basic Writings* (New York: Columbia University Press, 1963), "The Regulations of a King," 39.

13. D.C. Lau, trans., *Lao Tzu: Tao Te Ching* (Baltimore: Penguin Books, 1963) LXXVII, 140.

14. Chan, trans., *Instructions for Practical Living and Other Neo-Confucian Writings by Wang Yang-ming* (New York: Columbia University Press, 1963). 1. 21, 27.

15. *Analects* II:4.

16. Chan, *Instructions for Practical Living*, 2.156, 135.

17. On permanent revolution, see Stuart Schram, "Mao Tse-tung and the Theory of Permanent Revolution, 1958–69," *China Quarterly* 46 (April–June 1971): 221–224.

18. John Plamenatz, *Man and Society* (New York: McGraw-Hill, 1969), II: 393 ff.

19. Zhu Xi, *Hui'an xiansheng Zhu Wengong wenji* (Collection of literary works of Master Zhu), in *Sibu congkan*, XXXIII, 70.24a, quoted in Donald J. Munro, *Images of Human Nature: A Sung Portrait* (Princeton: Princeton University Press, 1988), 165.

20. The *Four Books* are the *Analects*, *Mencius*, *Great Learning*, and *Doctrine of the Mean*.

21. Munro, *Images*, 165–166.

22. Ibid., 170.

23. The translation is by K. J. DeWoskin and J. I. Crump in *In Search of the Supernatural: The Written Record* (Stanford: Stanford University Press, 1996), 128. The tale is from a work based on the *Sou-shen ji* (In search of the supernatural), attributed to Gan Bao (fl. A.D. 320), and the edition they used is the best known one, published in 1603, ch. 11, item 273.

24. Ray Huang, *1587: A Year of No Significance: The Ming Dynasty in Decline* (New Haven: Yale University Press, 1981), 89. See also 63, 77, 90.

25. Peter Railton, personal conversation.

26. Chan, *Instructions for Practical Living,* 2.175, n.11., 162.

27. Ibid. 3.226, 201, and 1.5, 11.

28. William T. Rowe, *Hankow: Commerce and Society in a Chinese City 1796–1889* (Stanford: Stanford University Press, 1984), 61.

29. Thomas A. Metzger, "The Organizational Capabilities of the Ch'ing State in the Field of Commerce: The Liang-huai salt Monopoly 1740–1840," in William E. Willmott, ed., *Economic Organization in Chinese Society* (Stanford: Stanford University Press, 1972), 9–45.

30. Ibid., 45.

31. Ibid., 40.

32. Susan Mann, *Local Merchants and the Chinese Bureaucracy, 1750–1950* (Stanford: Stanford University Press, 1987), 19.

33. Chin-keong Ng, *Trade and Society: The Amoy Network on the China Coast, 1683–1735* (Singapore: Singapore University Press, 1983), 60.

34. Shiba Yoshinobu, *Commerce and Society in Sung China,* trans. Mark Elvin (Ann Arbor: University of Michigan, Center for Chinese Studies, 1970), 212.

35. Pierre-Etienne Will, "State Intervention in the Administration of a Hydraulic Infrastructure: The Example of Hubei Province in Late Imperial Times," in Stuart R. Schram, ed., *The Scope of State Power in China* (London: School of Oriental and African Studies, 1985), 295, 309, 315.

36. Yen-p'ing Hao, *The Comprador in Nineteenth Century China: Bridge Between East and West* (Cambridge MA.: Harvard University Press, 1970), 149.

37. Inspired by some teachings of Mozi (fl 479–438 B.C.), they flourished during the Warring States period, working on issues in the philosophy of language and logic, among other things.

38. I am indebted to Brook Ziporyn for this point.

Notes to Chapter Two

1. James Reardon-Anderson, *The Study of Change: Chemistry in China, 1840–1949* (Cambridge: Cambridge University Press, 1991), 116.

2. Ibid., 214.

3. Mary Brown Bullock, *An American Transplant: The Rockefeller Foundation and Peking Union Medical College* (Berkeley: University of California Press, 1980), 80.

4. William C. Kirby, *Germany and Republican China* (Stanford: Stanford University Press, 1984), 206.

5. Zhang Dongsun (1886–1962) was a professor of philosophy at Yanjing University. Zhang developed a system that he calls epistemological pluralism. He rejected the division of knowledge between that which is given to the senses and the innate. Mind and its contents are cultural products. Key-chong Yap argues "that he was probably the only serious contemporary Chinese thinker who sought to develop an epistemology almost completely based on modern and contemporary Western sources." See his "Western Wisdom in the Mind's Eye of

a Westernized Chinese Lay Buddhist: The Thought of Chang Tung-sun (1886–1962)," Ph.D. dissertation, University of Oxford, 1989, "Introduction", 2. Jin Yuelin (1895–1984), a Professor of Philosophy at Peking University, was a student of Bertrand Russell. His philosophy combines naive realism with Kantian epistemology. His work *Lun dao* (On the Tao) contains a critique of the Chinese penchant for uniting heaven and man, with its attendant application of human values to nature. Consistent with this, he would oppose the idea of knowing as emotionally embodying the object of knowledge. His major work is *Zhishilun* (A theory of knowledge) (Beijing: Shangwu yinshuguan, 1983).

6. The phrase "xing yi zhi nan" (Action is easy; knowledge is difficult) is the subtitle of *Sun wen xueshuo* (Writings of Sun Yat-sen), completed in 1918–1919. Note that commentators sometimes reverse the order: Knowledge is difficult, action is easy (KDAE). See *Sun Zhongshan quanshu* (Complete works of Sun Yat-sen) (Guangzhou: Guangyi shuju, 1936), vol. II. This work is the primary source for his political epistemology and had a major impact on Chiang Kai-shek. Not all editions carry Sun's "Autobiographical Note" *(zixu)* to this work, which contains the clearest statement of Sun's Confucian-style voluntarism. So I also refer readers to a publication that does contain it: *Sun Wen xueshuo* (Taipei: Zhongyang wenwu gongyingshe, 1957), 1.

7. He Lin, "Zhi xing wenti di taolun yu fahui" (A discussion and elaboration of the question of knowledge and action), in He Lin, *Dangdai Zhongguo zhexue* (Contemporary Chinese philosophy), in *Zichan jieji xueshu sixiang pipan cankao ziliao,* IV (Source materials for the critique of capitalist academic thought), henceforth *ZJXSP* (Beijing: Shangwu yinshuguan, 1959), 70–116, especially 76. See also ch. 5 of *Sun Wen xueshuo.*

8. Sun uses this expression regularly. For example, at the beginning of chapter 8 of *Sun Wen xueshuo* he speaks of the tasks that can be successfully completed when such elite knowers fix their commitments to goals.

9. Henceforth, much of the source material used in this study comes from a compilation of major articles from newspapers, journals, and books between 1919–1949. The identification of sources was initiated in 1958 by the Philosophy Department at Peking University. The project was finally published in two units in 1981 and 1984 by the Philosophy Section of Liaoning University. The material is comprehensive, including works by heterodox Marxists such as Chen Duxiu and all notable nonMarxists, philosophers such as Zhang Zhunmai and Hu Shi and political figures such as Chiang Kai-shek and Chen Lifu. Full documentation on the original source is provided. The collection is divided by subject matter (philosophical school, topic of debate) and has an index by topic and by individual author. The two works are: *Zhongguo xiandai zhexue shi ziliao huibian* (Compilation of source materials in the history of modern Chinese philosophy), henceforth, *ZLHB* and *Zhongguo xiandai zhexue shi ziliao huibian xuji* (Continuation of the compilation of source materials in the history of modern Chinese philosophy), henceforth, *ZLHBXJ*. For a discussion of Sun's division of those who know from those who act, see Ai Siqi, "'*Zhongguo zhi mingyun'*—Jiduan weixinlun de yumin zhexue," ('China's Destiny'—An extremely idealistic

philosophy that stupifies the masses), *Jiefang ribao,* August 13, 1943, quoted in *ZLHB* 3, II, 32.

10. *Sun Zhongshan quan shu,* II, 35.

11. Quoted in Huang Wenshan, *Weishenglun de lishiguan* (The historical perspective of vitalism) (Taibei: Shangwu yinshuguan, 1982), 28.

12. Zhongguo guomindang zhongyang weiyuanhui, *San min zhuyi* (The Three People's Principles) (Taibei: Zhongyang wenwu gongyingshe, 1985), 227–32.

13. Ai Siqi, "Sun Zhongshan xiansheng de zhexue sixiang" (The philosophical thought of Mr. Sun Yat-sen"), originally in *Jiefang* 33 (April 1938), quoted in *ZLHB* 3, II, 38. See also Li Zehou, *Zhongguo jindai sixiang shi lun* (Essays on the history of modern Chinese philosophy) (Beijing: Xinhua shuju, 1986), 374.

14. Hu Shi, "Zhi nan, xing yi bu yi—Sun Zhongshan xiansheng de 'Xing yi zhi nan'shuo shuping" (If knowledge is difficult, action also is not easy—A review of Mr. Sun Yat-sen's theory that 'action is easy and knowledge is difficult'), in R*enquan lunji* (1931): 8, quoted in *ZLHBXJ*, XVI, 209.

15. Sun Yatsen's "Autobiographical Note" to *Sun Wen xueshuo.*

16. There is a lengthy explanation of Sun's position plus extensive quotations in He Lin, "Zhi xing wenti de taolun yu fahui." (A discussion and elaboration on the question of knowldge and action), *ZJXSP*, 50–69.

17. Chiang Kai-Shek, *Jiang Jieshi quanji* (The Collected Works of Chiang Kai-shek) (Shanghai: Wenhua bianyi guan, 1937), henceforth *JJQJ*, Part I, "The Principle of the Party," 69.

18. Ibid., 72.

19. Ibid., Part IV, "Education and Cultivation," 157.

20. Ibid., 114.

21. Chiang Kai-shek, *Zhongguo zhi mingyun* (China's destiny) (Chongqing: Zhongzheng shuju, 1943), 162.

22. He Lin traces this reworking by Chiang of Sun's ideas to Chiang's December, 1925 "Preface" to a piece written on behalf of the third class of the Huangpu Military Academy. See He Lin, "Zhi xing wenti" in *ZJXSP*, 115.

23. Chiang Kai-shek, "Xing de daoli" (The principle of practice), originally in *Lixing Zhexue* (1940 edition), quoted in *ZLHB* 3, II, 100–106.

24. Chiang Kai-shek, "Zhexue yu jiaoyu duiyu qingnian de guanxi" (The relationship of philosophy and education to the youth), originally presented on July 9–10, 1941, to a central administrative meeting of youth organizations, quoted in *ZLHB*, 3, II, 112–13.

25. Lin Jianhan, "Zhongcai xing de jexue tanyuan," (An exploration of the Director-General's philosophy of 'practice'), originally in *Shidai jingshen* 3 (1943), *juan* 7 quoted in *ZLHB* 3, II, 203.

26. Chiang Kai-shek, "Xing de daoli," *ZLHB* 3, II, 102.

27. There is a discussion of this in Hu Yiquan, "Lixing zhexue zhi xin jijie" (A new appreciation of the philosophy of practice), originally in *Wenhua xianfeng* 9 (1943), *juan* 2; see *ZLHB* 3, II, 137.

28. Quoted in He Lin, "Zhixing wenti," in *ZJXSP*, 110. See also Chiang Kai-shek, "Xiang de daoli" in *ZLHB* 3, II, 101. He made the point in a 1936 speech.

29. Ai Siqi, "Zhongguo zhi mingyun" in *ZLHB* 3, II, 29.

30. Quoted in He Lin, "Zhi xing wenti," in *ZJXSP*, 70.

31.Chiang Kai-shek, "Xing de daoli" in *ZLHB* 3, II, 101–102.

32.Chiang Kai-shek, "Zhexue yu jiaoyu," in *ZLHB*, 3, II, 107.

33. Ibid., 113.

34. Sidney H. Chang and Ramon H. Myers eds., *The Storm Clouds Clear Over China: The Memoirs of Ch'en Li-fu, 1900–1993* (Stanford: Hoover Institution Press, 1994), 248.

35. Tang Yijie of Peking University's Philosophy Department has edited a new volume that contains both the original literary Chinese version and later vernacular Chinese translation of Xiong's most famous work. See Xiong Shili, *Xin weishilun* (New idealism) (Beijing: Zhonghua shuju, 1985). It contains a photo of Xiong and Dong Biwu together.

36. Xiong Shili, *Shili yuyao* (Essential words of Xiong Shili) in *Shili congshu* (Complete reprinted works of Xiong Shili) (Taibei: Guangwen shuju, 1962), 4, 56b–57a.

37. Xiong Shili, *Zhongguo lishi jianghua* (Lectures on the history of China) (Taibei: Ming wen shuju, reprint of the 1939 edition), 10, 29.

38. Ibid., 36.

39. Xiong Shili, *Xin weishilun* (New idealism) (Taibei: Guangwen shuju, 1962) 8:62b.

40. Xiong Shili, *Ming xin pian* (Essay on the mind) (Taibei Xuesheng shuju, 1976), 67.

41. Ibid., 125, 129, 189.

42. Ibid., 136.

43. Ibid., 135, 144–45, and *Shili yuyao*, 3:27–28.

44. Xiong, *Ming xin pian*, 115, 125.

45. Ibid., 145.

46. Ibid., 134.

47. Ibid., 135.

48. Xiong, *Shili yuyao*, 1: 49a.

49. Ibid., 1: 49b.

50. Ibid., 1: 50a.

51. Chen Lifu, *Sheng zhi yuanli* (The original principle of life) (1944; rpt. Taibei: Zhengzhong shuju, 1964), 149.

52. Ibid., 20.

53. Ibid., 156.

54. Ibid., 180–85.

55. Feng Weiguo, "Lixing zhexue yu lunli gaizao" (The philosophy of practice and the reform of ethics), originally in *Xin renshi* 1941.11: 15, in *ZLHBXJ*, 18, 34.

56. Chen Lifu, "Zhanshi jiaoyu shishi fang'an gangyao" (An outline of principles for implementing education at various levels during wartime), in Qin

Xiaoyi ed., *Zhanshi jiaoyu fangzhen* (Guiding principles for wartime education) (Taibei: Zhongyang wenwu gongyingshe, 1976), 306–307.

57. Chen Lifu, "Minzu shengcun de yuan dongji" (The original motive force of the people's existence) in ZLHB 2, VII, 26.

58. He Lin's most comprehensive essay on this is "Zhixing wenti" in *ZJXSP*, 70–116. However, there are many others. See the index to *ZLHB*, 3, V.

59. He Lin, "Dushu yu sixiang" (Reading and thinking) in *Wenhua yu rensheng* (Culture and life) (Taibei: Beiping xian chubanshe, 1973), 255. On the use of models in self-cultivation, see 138–39.

60. See the first chapter of his *Dangdai Zhongguo zhexue.*

61. In the 1947 edition, He Lin devotes the fourth section of *Dangdai Zhongguo zhexue* to "Zhengtong zhexue yu Sanmin zhuyi zhexue de fazhan" (Orthodox philosophy and the development of the philosophy of the Three People's Principles).

62. He Lin, "Jindai weixinlun jianshi" (A brief interpretation of modern idealism), in *Zhexue yu zhexueshi lunwenji* (Collection of works on philosophy and the history of philosophy) (1934; rpt. Beijing: Sangwu yinshuguan, 1990), 135.

63. He Lin, "Shidai sichao de yanbian yu pipan" (The evolution and critique of thought trends of the times), *Dangdai Zhongguo zhexue*, 68–69.

64. He Lin, "Shikong yu chao shikong" (Space and time and transcending space and time), originally in *Zhexue pinglun* 1940.4 *juan* 7 in *ZLHB* 3, V, 123–39.

65. He Lin devotes the first chapter of his *Dangdai Zhongguo zhexue* to tracing the influence of Wang Yangming on twentieth-century figures.

66. *ZLHB*, 3, V, 1–205.

67. Zhang Xuezhi, "Lun He Lin dui Sibinnuosha (Spinoza) sixiang de xishou yu gaizao" (He Lin's absorbtion from and reformulation of Spinoza's thought), *Wen shi zhe* (Journal of literature, history, and philosophy) (Shandong), 1990.1: 34–39.

68. He Lin, "Jindai weixinlun jianshu" (A sketch of modern idealism) in *ZJXSP*, 123. Xie Youwei cites this as a core idea in his review of this work, "He wei weixinlun?" (What is idealism?), originally in *Sixiang yu shidai* 1943.11, in *ZLHB*, 3, V, 201.

69. He Lin, "Wulun guandian de xin jiantao" (A new investigation of the concept of the five relationships), originally in *Wenhua yu rensheng* 11 (1947), in *ZLHB* 3, V, 78.

70. He Lin, "Songru de sixiang fangfa" ("The thinking methods of the Song Confucians") in *ZJXSP*, 186, 192.

71. Zhang Xuezhi, "Lun He Lin de 'Xi zhe Dong zhe, xin tong li tong'" (On He Lin's 'Merging of Western and Chinese philosophy and equation of mind and principle'), unpublished paper, 12.

72. Xie Youwei, "He wei weixinlun?," in *ZLHB*, 3, V, 201.

73. He Lin, "Shikong yu chao shikong," in *ZLHB*, 3, V, 137.

74. He Lin, *Zhexue yu zhexueshi lun wenji*, 184–85.

75. Ibid., 659–60.

76. Zhang Xuezhi, "Lun He Lin de 'xi zhe dong zhe, xin tong li tong,'" 14.

77. He discusses this in *Heige'er (Hegel) zhexue yanjin ji* (Collected works on the evolution of Hegel's philosophy) (Shanghai: Renmin chuban she, 1986).

78. Guy S. Alitto, *The Last Confucian* (Berkeley: University of California Press, 1979).

79. Sin-yee Chan, "The Concepts of Intuition and *Li-hsing* in Liang Shuming's Philosophy," M.A. thesis, University of Michigan, 1990.

80. Liang Shuming, *Xiangcun jianshe lilun* (The theory of rural construction; 1934), in Liang Shuming, *Liang Shuming xueshu jinghua lun* (A record of the core scholarly teachings of Liang Shuming) (Beijing: Beijing shifan xueyuan chubanshe, 1988), 504.

81. Ibid., 505.

82. Ai Siqi, "'Zhongguo zhi mingyun'" in *ZLHB* 3, II, 24–33.

83. Franz Schurman, *Ideology and Organization in China* (Berkeley: University of California Press, 1966), xxxii.

Notes to Chapter Three

1. Mao Zedong, "Yanjiu lunxianqu" (An investigation of enemy-held territory) (1939), in *ZXZJC*.II, 995.

2. Ibid.

3. Mao Zedong, "Ziyou shi biran de renshi he shijie de gaizao" (Freedom is knowledge of necessity and changing the world) (1941), in *ZXZJC*, II, 998.

4. Mao Zedong, "Guan yu nongcun diaocha" (On the investigation of rural villages) (1941), in *ZXZJC*, II, 1003–04.

5. Mao Zedong, "'Qida' gongzuo fangzhen" (Work guidelines for the Seventh All-Peoples Congress) (1945), in *ZXZJC*, II, 1019.

6. Maurice Meisner, *Mao's China and After* (New York: The Free Press, 1986), 41.

7. "Some Questions Concerning Methods of Leadership," (1943) in *Selected Works of Mao Zedong*, (Beijing: Foreign Languages Press, 1965), 3, 119.

8. Li Zhisui, *The Private Life of Chairman Mao*, trans., Tai Hung-chao with editorial ssistance of Anne F. Thurston, (New York: Random House, 1994), 296.

9. Ibid., 308, 319.

10. Among the critics in the 1950s was Bo Yibo, who chaired the State Economic Commission. See ibid., 308.

11. Meisner, 148–51.

12. Li Zhisui, 131.

13. Mao Zedong, "Reading Notes on the Soviet Union's Political Economy," in *Joint Publications Research Service (JPRS)* 61269–2, February 20, 1974, 282.

14. Li Zhisui, 274.

15. *Renmin Ribao (RMRB) (People's Daily)* October 13, 1983.

16. Ibid.

17. Song Renqiong, "Yong xin dangzhang jiaoyu dangyuan, wei zhengdang zuohao sixiang zhunbei" (Use new Party rules to educate Party members,

do a good job of thought preparation for the entire Party), in *Hongqi* (Red flag) 1982. 24: 19.

18. *RMRB*, October 13, 1983.

19. Ibid.

20. *Zhongbao yuekan* (Zhongbao monthly) (Hong Kong) 1986.75: 7933.

21. Deng Xiaoping, "Wuzhi wenming yu jingshen wenming" (Material civilization and spiritual civilization), in *Deng Xiaoping wenxuan* (Selected writings of Deng Xiaoping) (Beijing: Renmin chubanshe, 1983), 326.

22. Li Zhisui, 234.

23. Ibid., 136.

24. Ma Yinchu, *Xin renkou lun* (A new theory of population) (Beijing: Beijing chubanshe, 1979), 2.

25. Ma Yinchu, "Woguo renkou wenti yu fazhan shengchanli de guanxi" (The relation between our country's population and the development of productive capacity), in ibid., 26–29. Originally published in *Dagongbao*, May 9, 1957.

26. Yang Jianye, *Ma Yinchu zhuan* (Biography of Ma Yinchu), (Beijing: Zhongguo qingnian chubanshe, 1986), 159, 161–63.

27. Ibid., 162.

28. Ibid., 155. This work originally appeared in *RMRB*, July 5, 1957.

29. Ma Yinchu, *Xin renkou lun*, 11, 14, 18.

30. Yang Jianye, 157.

31. Ma Yinchu, "Wo guo renkou wenti," 28.

32. Yang Jianye, 168.

33. Jiang Shan, *Maersasi "Renkou lun" he "Xin renkou lun" de piping* (A critique of Malthus's "Theory of Population" and of "A New Theory of Population) (Shanghai: Shanghai renmin chubanshe, 1958), 58. For other critiques, see 60–63, and Yang Jianye, 169.

34. Jiang Shan, 62–63.

35. John E. Besemeres, *Socialist Population Politics* (New York: M.E. Sharpe, 1980), 20–26.

36. Jiang Shan, *Maersasi "Renkou lun" he "Xin renkou lun" de piping*, 66–68.

37. Yang Jianye, 238–39.

38. "Bohai erhao zuanjingchuan fanchen shigu shuomingle shemma?" (What does the sinking of the Bohai No. 2 platform explain?), in *Xinhua yuekan* (New China Monthly) (Beijing) 1980.7: 132.

39. Ibid., 133.

40. For example, it was a "great campaign" (*da hui zhan*), meaning that all specialists could be diverted from other projects to work on it. "King of the mountain competitions" (*dalei biwu*) could take place between workers, wherein losers tumble to the bottom and lose their privileges. See "Song Zhenming jiu 'Bohai erhao' zuanjingchuan fanchen shigu de jiantao" (Song Zhenming's self-criticism concerning the Bohai No.2 platform), in *Xinhua yuekan* 1980.8: 71.

41. "Bohai erhao zuanjingchuan fanchen shigu shuomingle shemma?" 133.

42. "Song Zhenming jiu 'Bohai erhao,'" in *Xinhua yuekan* 1980.8: 71.

43. "Shenke de jiaoxun" (A profound lesson), in *Xinhua yuekan* 1980.8: 69.

44. Ibid.

45. Ze Ming, "Refutation of 'Practice is the only source of knowledge,'" originally in *Shehui kexue* 2 (1980), and quoted in Kalpana Misra, "Rethinking Marxism in Post-Mao China: The Erosion of Official Ideology, 1978–84." Ph.D. diss, University of Michigan, 1992, 122.

46. Helen E. Longino, *Science as Social Knowledge* (Princeton: Princeton University Press, 1990), 12.

Notes to Chapter Four

1. Reardon-Anderson, 202.

2. Daniel W.Y. Kwok, *Scientism in Chinese Thought 1900–1950* (New Haven: Yale University Press, 1965), 22–23.

3. Reardon-Anderson, 203.

4. Ibid., 204. He refers to Charlotte Furth's article "Intellectual Change: From the Reform Movement to the May Fourth Movement, 1895–1920," in *The Cambridge History of China*, XII, 351–361.

5. Reardon-Anderson, 208.

6. Ibid., 213.

7. Li Xinsheng and Li Xiaolu, "Jiazhi fanwei yingyinru renshilun" (Introducing the category of value into epistemology), in *Huanan shifan daxue xuebao* (Journal of South China Normal University) 1987.1:2. Another fairly typical position is encountered in such words as these: "human knowledge is always a union of factual and value knowledge" and "human knowledge definitely cannot be limited to factual knowledge," wherein scientific and political values are confused in these uses of the term value. We know this because the author states that the test of whether or not a theory or knowledge has any vitality is a function of whether or not it can serve *practice*, that is whether or not it can satisfy a material or spiritual need of society or a subject. See Zheng Guoping, "Jiazhi zai renshizhong de zuoyong" (The function of value in knowing), in *Zhexue yanjiu* (Philosophical Investigations) 1986.7: 29.

8. Ibid., 28.

9. Yuan Guiren, "Jiazhi yu renshi" (Values and cognition), in *Beijing shifandaxue xuebao* (Journal of Beijing Normal University) 1985.3: 50, 54.

10. Ibid., 54.

11. Zhou Guoping, "Ren de huodong he wanzheng de renxing" (Human activity and the integrative nature of man), in *Rendao zhuyi wenti wenji* (Collection of problems in humanism) (Liaoning: Liaoning renmin chubanshe, 1985), 123.

12. Zheng Guoping, 29.

13. Chiang Kai-shek, "Xing de daoli" (The principle of practice), in *Zhongguo xiandai zhexueshi jiaoxue cailiao xuanji* (Selected academic source materials for the study of the history of modern Chinese philosophy) (Beijing: Beijing daxue chubanshe, 1988) II, 943–944.

14. Hu Haibo, "Shehui zhuti huodong de fangfalun gouxiang" (Thinking through the methodology [for research] on the activity of social subjects), *Dong-*

bei shifan daxue xuebao (Journal of Northeast China Normal University), 1989.1: 10.

15. Lin Fang, *Xinling de kunhuo yu zijiu* (The puzzle and salvation of the psyche) (Liaoning: Liaoning renmin chubanshe, 1989), 348.

16. Lin Fang, "Makesi zhuyi he renben xinlixue" (Marxism and humanistic psychology), in *Xinlixue xuebao* (Journal of psychology) 1982.2: 13. The leading philosopher, Zhang Dainian, wrote in 1990 that "everyone agrees that some needs are superior to others." See "On Levels of Values" in *Social Sciences in China* 1990.4, 24.

17. Lin Fang, "Comments on Western Humanistic Psychology,' in *Social Sciences in China* 1985.3: 171.

18. Lin Fang, *Xinling*, 348.

19. Lin Fang, "Makesi zhuyi ho renben xinlixue," 10–12.

20. Pan Shu, *Xinlixue jianzha* (Psychological notes) (Beijing: Renminjiaoyu chubanshe, 1984), 65–67.

21. Ibid., 67.

22. Lin Fang, *Xinling*, 346–348.

23. Pan Shu, "Jiajin gaizao xinlixue, wei quanmian kaichuang shehui zhuyi xiandaihua jianshe de xinjumian fuwu" (Speed up the reconstruction of psychology in order to serve the new situation in the construction of socialist modernization), in *Xinli kexue tongxun* (Psychological sciences review) 1983.2: 8.

24. Zhang Shiying, "Xifang zhexueshizhong zhutixing yuanze de fazhan yu Zhongguo zhexueshizhong guanyu ren de lilun" (The development of the principle of subjectivity in the history of Western philosophy, and the theory of man in the history of Chinese philosophy), in *Ren yu ziran* (Man and nature) Philosophy Department of Pekjing University, ed., (Beijing: Beijing daxue chubanshe, 1987), 97.

25. Alison H. Black, *Man and Nature in the Philosophical Thought of Wang Fu-chih* (Seattle: University of Washington Press, 1989), 159–163.

26. Feng Youlan, *Xin lixue* (New rationalistic philosophy), in *Feng Youlan xueshu jinghua lu* (A record of the scholarly essentials of Feng Youlan) (Beijing: Beijing shifan xueyuan chubanshe, 1988), 357.

27. I am grateful to many participants in the conference, "Fusion and Innovation of Chinese and Western Philosophy and Culture," an International Symposium for the Centenary of the Birth of Mr. Feng Youlan, held at Tsinghua University in Beijing, December 16–20, 1995. They helped me clarify Feng's positions on a number of points. I would like to mention especially Mr. Meng Peiyuan of the Institute of Philsophy of the Chinese Academy of the Social Sciences and Dr. Alexander V. Lomanov of the Institute of Far Eastern Studies of the Russian Academy of Sciences. Dr. Lomanov provided me with the specifics on Feng's relations to the Vienna Circle. These include such facts as Feng's 1933 visit to Wittgenstein, his affirmation of Wittgenstein's desire to explain metaphysics rather than eliminate it, and his 1943 article entitled, "Xin lixue zai zhexue zhong zhi diwei ji qi fangfa" (The position and methodology of New Rationalism in philosophy), that appeared in *Zhexue pinlun* 8, 1943. Therein Feng specifically says that he does not share the methodology of the Vienna Circle or its position

on metaphysics. Real philosophy should focus on principle (*li*), not simply on the separation of names or clarification.

28. Feng Youlan, *Sansong tang zixu* (My intellectual autobiography) (Beijing: Sanlian shushe, 1984), 246–247. Also found *in Feng Youlan xueshu jinghua lu*, 423.

29. Feng Youlan, *Zhongguo Zhexueshi xinbian* (New edition of the history of Chinese philosophy), in *Feng Youlan xueshu jinghua lu*, I, 523–524.

30. Ibid., 525. Feng's interest in distinguishing the objective from the subjective in the 1980s is paired with his wish to turn the Confucian legacy away from the fact-value fusion in descriptions of the natural world. In 1986, in his revised *History of Chinese Philosophy*, he criticized Zhu Xi for confusing fact and value. He said that Zhu's idea of "sudden insight" into the integrated principles of all things is a *value* concept. That concept "cannot be reached through the method of increasing [objective] knowledge." Feng Youlan, *Zhongguo zhexueshi xinbian* (New edition of the history of Chinese philosophy), Volume 5 (of 7) (Beijing: Renmin chubanshe, 1988), 177-178.

31. Li Zhilin, "Lun Zhongguo quantong siwei fangshi de liangchongxing ji biange de nanjuxing" (On the twofold character of traditional Chinese thinking and the difficulties in reforming it), in *Zhexue yanjiu*, 1989.7: 22–23.

32. Yu Qiming, "Shehui kexue lilun de zhenli yiyi ji qi panding," (On the meaning and determination of truth in theories in the social sciences), *Beijing shifan daxue xuebao*, 1990.5: 47.

33. Chen Zhonghua and Wang Wenyang, "Luelun jishu de jiazhi chidu" (Brief discussion on the value-measure of technology), in *Beijing shifan daxue xuebao*, 1987.2: 59–62.

34. Wang Meng, "Dongtian de huati" (A winter's tale), *Xiaoshuojia* (Fiction writer), 1985.2: 203-226.

35. Ibid., 204.

36. Ibid., 207.

37. Ibid., 226.

38. Cited in Donald J. Munro, "One-Minded Hierarchy versus Interest Group Pluralism: Two Chinese approaches to Conflict," in William Zimmerman and Harold Jacobson, eds., *New Approaches to Conflict in World Politics* (Ann Arbor: University of Michigan Press, 1994), 256–257. Original citation from *Foreign Broadcast Information Service* (*FBIS*), China, August 19, 1987, K12.

39. Zimmerman and Jacobson, 262.

Notes to Chapter Five

1. Zhang Shiying, "Xifang zhexueshi," 83.

2. The immediate stimulus for open discussion of subjectivity was the politically inspired topic, the criterion of truth, which aimed at undercutting the supreme authority of Mao. This opened the door to the topic of practice (something akin to what a Western philosopher would call "operations"), a standard technical term in Marxist epistemology. This in turn raised the question as to how much the investigator's values or needs affect his experience in prac-

tice. The philosopher Li Zehou and literary critic Liu Zaifu were the first to raise the issue of subjectivity, though the philosopher Mou Zongsan traces it to Wang Yangming. Li's influential work at that time was *Pipan zhexue de pipan* (*A critique of critical philosophy*), 1979, dealing with Kant, among other things. He maintained that over time, people internally transform external impressions, and those transformed impressions eventually play a role in how they change the world. This opposes the Leninist theory of the mind as passive reflector.

3. Wang Ruoshui's articles containing these citations appeared in Shanghai's *Wenhuibao*, July 17 and 18, 1986. They were translated in *FBIS*, China, July 23 and 24, 1986. The citations appear on pages K8 and K12 for July 23, and K5 for July 24.

4. Hu Qiaomu's contrasting position appeared in *Hongqi* (Red Flag) 1984.2: 2–28 as "Guanyu rendaozhuyi he yihua wenti" (On the question of humanism and alienation). My reference is to passages on page 20.

5. Therefore, the subject creates the world, so to speak, and objectivity changes as subjects change or as subjects with different interests do the knowing. A fine example of the confusion of scientific value with moral or political value can be found in Zheng Guoping, "Jiazhi zai renshi zhong de zuoyong" (The function of values in knowing), in *Zhexue yanjiu* 1986.7: 28–29. See also Wang Pengling, "Mianxiang zhuti he kexue" (Toward the Subject and Science), in *Zhongguo shuhui kexue* (*Social Sciences in China*), Chinese version, 1987.3: 68–72. Translated as "Toward the Subject and Science: Two Tendencies in the Study of Dialectical Materialism in China over the Past Decade" in *Social Sciences in China* 1988.2: 9–16. See especially 9–10. See also Li Deshun, "On the Unity of Truth and Value," in *Social Sciences in China* 1985.4: 147–148.

As Li Zehou explains it, interpretive paradigms are molded ("sedimented") in people's consciousness over the course of history. The subjectivity topics that took this route fit within the subfield of epistemology. For an English language reference to this topic, see Li Zehou, "The Philosophy of Kant and a Theory of Subjectivity" in A. T. Tymieniecka, ed., *Analecta Husserliana* 21: 135–149, especially 137 (Leiden: Reidel, 1986). Strictly speaking, writers should use the term *zhuguanxing* for this theme, but they rarely do, preferring the topical favorite, *zhutixing*.

6. Guo Zhan, "The Course of Human Subjectivity," in *Social Sciences in China* 1987.4: 209.

7. Ibid. [Translation revised].

8. Yang Shi, "The Historical Status of the Traditional Chinese Theory of Man," in *Social Sciences in China* 1989.4: 55.

9. Personal discussions, winter 1993.

10. Lin Fang, "Comments on Western Humanistic Psychology," 59.

11. Lin Fang, *Xinling de kunhuo yu zijiu*, 302, 326–327.

12. Li Deshun, "On the Unity of Truth and Value," 142. Also, Wang Pengling, "Towards the Subject and Science," 10.

13. One of the main popularizers of this idea was the former *People's Daily* editor Wang Ruoshui. For an easily accessible version of some of his views, see note 3 to this chapter.

14. Liu Zaifu, *Lun wenxue de zhutixing* (On subjectivity in literature) (Ha'erbin: Heilongjiang jiaoyu chubanshe, 1988), 73 and 79–80.

15. Wang Penglin, "Toward the Subject and Science" in *Social Sciences in China* 1988.2: 9.

16. Originally a Song period expression.

18. An individual who interviewed the editors in charge of *China Youth* (*Zhongguo qingnian,* henceforth *ZGQN*) in 1980 reports the following. Several letters from youthful readers dealt with the theme of individuals choosing their own life activities. The editors pasted sections of the different letters together to make one "reader's" letter. The publication of this stimulated the avalanche of 60,000 letters referred to below.

19. Gui Yang et al, "Women shehui zhong ren zemma yang bei 'moshihua'le" (How the people in our society have been 'standardized'), in *ZGQN* 1980.9:12–14. Also "Rensheng de yiyi jiujing shi shemma?" (What, after all, is the meaning of human life?), editorial, in *ZGQN* 1980.5: 2–5, especially 4. See also "Shemma shi kexue de geming renshengguan?" (What is the scientific revolutionary view of life?), editorial, in *ZGQN* 1980.7: 4–6. Citation is on 5.

20. "Chengcai" (Becoming an accomplished person), editorial, in *ZGQN* 1988.1: 2–5, especially 3.

21. Liu Baiwen et al., "Xiandai shehui: chongxin renzheng ziwo" (Contemporary society—A renewed authentication of the self), in *ZGQN* 1992.9: 12–13.

22. Ibid.

23. Wang Ruoshui has said this. But a good example of a popular statement on the matter is note 44 below.

24. See note 19 above.

25. "Rensheng de yiyi," 4.

26."Shemma shi kexue de geming renshengguan?" 5.

27. "Chengcai," 3.

28. "Xiangei rensheng yiyi de sikaozhe" (To those contemplating the meaning of life), editorial, *ZGQN* 1981.6: 2.

29. "Chengcai," 2–5.

30. "Shinian: Ai de songdong he tuijin" (The past ten years: flexibility and advances in 'love') *ZGQN* 1988.9: 3.

31. "Minzhu" (Democracy), *ZGQN* 1988.5: 4–7, especially 6.

32. Cong Weixi, "Fenglei yan" (Eyes with tears), in *Quanguo youxiu zhongpian xiaoshuo, 1985–86* (Collection of nation-wide prize-winning novellas, 1985–86) (Beijing: Zuojia chubanshe, 1988), 1056. Brought to my attention by An Yanming.

33. Han Jingting, "Shichang jiaoluo de huangdi" (The Emperor in the corner of the market), in *Quanguo youxiu zhongpian xiaoshuo, 1983–84* (Collection of nation-wide prize-winning novellas, 1983–84) (Beijing: Zuojia chubanshe, 1986), 1173–74. Brought to my attention by An Yanming.

34. Chu Wanzhong, "Lun ren de zhutixing de fazhan yu xiandai jiaoyu zhutixing yuanze de jianli" (On the development of subjectivity and the estab-

ishment of the principle of subjectivity in contemporary education), *Beijing shifan daxue xuebao* 1989.4: 75–81.

35. Ibid.

36. Tian Hanzu, "Lun xuesheng zhutixing zuoyong fahui de jiben yuanze" (On the basic principle of the function of giving play to the student's subjectivity), *Jiaoyu yanjiu* (Educational investigations) 1991.8: 117. Also Wang Kunqing, "Lun jiaoyu jiazhi zhong ren de jiazhi diwei" (On the position of human values within educational values) in *Huadong shifan daxue xuebao* (Journal of East China Normal University) 1991.2: 50–51.

37. Beijingshi jiaoyu kexue yanjiusuo (The Institute of Educational Science of Beijing), "Peiyang ershiyi shiji shehui zhuyi Zhongguo de zhuren" (Cultivating Socialist China's Masters of the Twenty-first Century) in Xiao Jingruo et al., eds., *Putong jiaoyu gaige* (The reform of ordinary education) Beijing: Renmin jiaoyu chubanshe, 1987, 230–245.

38. Ibid., 237.

39. Tian Hanzu, 117.

40. Zhou Haobo, "Shilun jiaoyu guocheng zhong de ertong zhutixing" (A tentative discussion into childhood subjectivity within the educational process), in *Jiaoyu yanjiu* 1989.6: 19.

41. Wang Daojun and Guo Wen'an, "Shilun jiaoyu de zhutixing" (A tentative discussion on subjectivity in education), *Huadong shifan daxue xuebao* 1990.4: 40.

42. Ibid.

43. Lu Xiangkang, "Jiaoyu dingze: Zhutixing he zhudaoxing de shixian" (A pedogogical rule: The appearance of subjectivity and dominance), *Huazhong shifan daxue xuebao* (Journal of Central China Teacher's College),1987.1: 60.

44. Yang Fan, "Shekou fengbo de qianqian houhou" (The before and after of a disturbance in Shekou), in *ZGON* 1988.8: 5.

45. Doyal and Harris, *Empiricism, Explanation, and Rationality*, 30–31.

46. Crombie, *Science, Optics and Music*, 356–357.

47. Longino, *Science as Social Knowledge*, 130.

48. Richard E. Neustadt and Ernest R. May, *Thinking in Time: The Uses of History for Decision Makers* (New York: The Free Press, 1986).

49. Longino, 76.

50. James Q. Wilson, *The Moral Sense* (New York: The Free Press, 1993), 200–207.

51. Ibid., 212–215.

52. Plamenatz, *Man and Society*, I:70–76.

53. Ibid., 77.

54. See Edwin Curley, ed., *Thomas Hobbes, Leviathan* (Indianapolis: Hackett, 1994), "Introduction." Brought to my attention by Mika Manty.

55. Frederic Wakeman, Jr. "The Civil Society and Public Sphere Debate," *Modern China* 19.2 (April 1993): 111 and 131.

56. Donald J. Munro, "One-Minded Hierarchy Versus Interest-Group Pluralism, 247–274.

57. Clement Mak alerted me to the role of tabloid newspapers in this regard. The impact of the government's decision to allow newsprint producers to sell some newsprint at market prices is reported in Pei Minxin, *From Reform to Revolution: The Demise of Communism in China and the Soviet Union* (Cambridge: Harvard University Press, forthcoming), chapter 5.

58. Arthur Danto, "Postscript," in Munro, *Individualism and Holism*, 389.

59. Immanuel Kant, *Foundations of the Metaphysics of Morals* in Lewis White Beck, ed., *Kant Selections* (New York: Macmillan, 1988), 268–270, lines 424–442. I am deeply grateful to Steven Darwall, David Hills, and Paul Frank for clarifying my understanding of Kant on some of these crucial issues.

60. Ibid., 276, line 433.

61. "What is Enlightenment?" 35, in Beck, line 462.

62. Ibid., 41, line 466.

63. John Herman Randall, Jr., *The Career of Philosophy: From the German Enlightenment to the Age of Darwin*, 2 vols. (New York: Columbia University Press, 1965), 2: 235, in Donald J. Munro, "Introduction," to Munro, *Individualism and Holism*, 3.

64. The complete break with this interest in any universal values is symbolized by Max Stirner's 1844 work, *The Ego and its Own: The Case of the Individual against Authority*, trans. S. T. Byington, 1907. Thanks to Paul Frank for bringing this to my attention.

65. See Munro, *Individualism and Holism*, "Acknowledgments," for the debt I owe to Steven Lukes, *Individualism*, (New York: Harper and Row, 1973). Lukes cites this passage in Lukes, 70.

66. Chan, trans., *Instructions for Practical Living*, 2.139, 108.

67. Ibid. 2.139, 109–110.

68. Ibid. 1.3, 7.

69. Ibid. 2.135, 99; 2.139, 109; 1.3, 7.

70. Ibid. 1.99, 61 and 1.101, 65.

Glossary

Ai Siqi	艾思奇
An Yanming	安延明
benlai ruci	本來如此
biantong	變通
bohai er hao	渤海 2 號
Cai Yuanpei	蔡元培
cha'e xuanju	差額選舉
Chen Lifu	陳立夫
Chen Yi	陳毅
cheng	誠
Cheng Yi	程頤
chuangzao-xing	創造性
da yitong	大一同
danwei	單位
daode	道德
Daqing	大慶
datong	大同
Dazhai	大寨
dong	動
Dong Biwu	董必武
duli sikao	獨立思考
dute	獨特
fanxing	範型
fen	分
Feng Youlan	馮友蘭
Fu Sinian	傅斯年
gan ziji xiang gan de shi	干自己想干的事
gong	公
guagou dan-wei	掛鉤單位
guantong	貫通
Guo Moruo	郭沫若
He Lin	賀麟
Hu Linyi	胡林翼
Hu Shi	胡適
Hu Yaobang	胡耀邦
hui	會
Huiyuan	慧遠
Jiang Menglin	蔣夢麟
Jiang Tingfu	蔣廷黻
Jin Yuelin	金岳霖
jingshi	經世
Kang Shi'en	康世恩
Kang Youwei	康有爲
kuzhan	苦戰
kuada zhu-guan neng-dongxing	夸大主觀能動性
Laozi	老子
Li Dazhao	李大釗
Liang Suming	梁漱溟
liangxin	良心
liangzhi	良知
Lin Biao	林彪
Lin Fang	林方
Liu Shaoqi	劉少奇
lixiang	理想
lixing (p. 38)	力行
lixing (p. 51)	理性
lizhi	理智
Ma Yinchu	馬演初
mofan	模範
moshihua	模式化
Mou Zongsan	牟宗三
mudi lun	目的論
muyuxue	沐浴學
nei	内
nengdongxing	能動性
Pan Shu	潘菽
qizhi	氣志

qu	趣
quanmian fazhan	全面發展
reqi	熱氣
ren	仁
ren duo shi haoshi	人多是好事
rujiang	儒將
saima	賽馬
shen de wenhua	神的文化
shiji	實際
shili	實理
sixiang juewu	思想覺悟
taiji	太極
Tang Junyi	唐君毅
teshu	特殊
ti	體
tianli	天理
ticha	體察
tongqing	同情
wai	外
Wang Fuzhi	王夫之
Wang Meng	王蒙
Wang Ruoshui	王若水
Wang Yangming	王陽明
Weisheng lun	唯生論
xiangma	相馬
xiangyue	鄉約
xin lixue	新理學
xing (p. 35)	行
xing (p. 22)	性
xinyi	心意
Xiong Shili	熊十力
xixin	習心
xuanze ziji de qiantu	選擇自己的前途
Yang Xianzhen	楊獻珍
yingdang ru ci	應當如此
yixin	一心
yong	用
you	有
you ganjin	有干勁
you ruiqi	有銳氣
yuzhou yizhi	宇宙意志
Zeng Guofan	曾國藩
Zhang Dongsun	張東蓀
Zhang Junmei	張君勱
Zhang Zhidong	張之洞
zhenji	眞際
zhi	智
zhi nan xing yi	知難行易
zhijue	直覺
zhishi	知識
zhixin	治心
Zhongyang zhengzhi xuexiao	中央政治學校
zhu	主
Zhu Xi	朱熹
zhuguan yizhi daiti keguan shiji	主觀意志代替客觀實際
zhuguanxing	主觀性
zhutixing	主體性
zi'ai	自愛
zili	自立
ziwo jiazhi	自我價值
ziwo xiuyang	自我修養
zixin	自信
zizhi	自治
zizhu	自主
zizhu huodong	自主活動
zizun	自尊
zuoren	作人

Works Cited

Ai Siqi 艾思奇. "Sun Zhongshan xiansheng de zhexue sixiang" 孫中山先生的哲學思想 (The philosophical thought of Mr. Sun Yat-sen). *Jiefang* 解放 33 (April 1938). See *ZLHB* 3, II, 33–41.

——. "*Zhongguo zhi mingyun*—Jiduan weixinlun de yumin zhexue" 中國之命運— 極端唯心論的愚民哲學 (*China' s Destiny*— An extremely idealistic philosophy that stupidifies the masses). *Jiefang ribao* 解放日報, August 13, 1943.

Alitto, Guy S. *The Last Confucian.* Berkeley: University of California Press, 1979.

Beijingshi jiaoyu kexue yanjiusuo 北京市教育科學研究所 (Beijing Institute of Educational Science). "Peiyang ershiyi shiji shehui zhuyi Zhongguo de zhuren" 培養二十一世紀社會主義中國的主人 (Cultivating the masters of socialist China in the twenty-first century). In *Putong jiaoyu gaige* 普通教育改革, Xiao Jingruo 肖敬若 et al., eds. Beijing: Renmin jiaoyu chubanshe, 1987, 230–245.

Besemeres, John E. *Socialist Population Politics.* New York: M.E. Sharpe, 1980.

Black, Alison H. *Man and Nature in the Philosophical Thought of Wang Fu-chih.* Seattle: University of Washington Press, 1989.

"Bohai erhao zuanjingchuan fanchen shigu shuomingle shemma? 渤海二號鑽井船翻沈事故說明了甚麼? (What does the sinking of the Bohai No. 2 platform explain?). *Xinhua yuebao* 新華月報 1980.7: 132–134.

Bullock, Mary Brown. *An American Transplant: The Rockefeller Foundation and Peking Union Medical College.* Berkeley: University of California Press, 1980.

Chan Sin-yee. "The Concepts of Intuition and *Li-hsing* in Liang Shu-ming' s Philosophy." M.A. thesis, University of Michigan, 1990.

Chan, Wing-tsit, trans. *Instructions for Practical Living and Other Neo-Confucian Writings by Wang Yang-ming.* New York: Columbia University Press, 1963.

Chang, Sidney H., and Ramon H. Myers, eds. *The Storm Clouds Clear Over China: The Memoirs of Ch' en Li-fu, 1900–1993.* Stanford: Hoover Institution Press, 1994.

Chen Lifu 陳立夫. *Sheng zhi yuanli* 生之原理 (The original principle of life). 1944. Reprint. Taibei: Zhengzhong shuju, 1964.

——. "Zhanshi geji jiaoyu shishi fang' an gangyao" 戰時各級教育實施方案綱要 (An outline of principles for the implementation of education at various levels during wartime). In *Zhanshi jiaoyu fangzhen* 戰時教育方針 (Guiding principles for wartime education). Qin Xiaoyi, ed. Taibei: Zhongyang wenwu gongyingshe, 1976, 1–47.

——. "Minzu shengcun de yuan dongji" 民族生存的原動機 (The original motive force of the people's existence) in ZLHB 2, VII, 26.

Chen Zhonghua 陳仲華, and Wang Wenyang 王文揚. "Luelun jishu de jiazhi chidu" 略論技術的價值尺度 (Brief discussion on the value-measure of technology). *Beijing shifan daxue xuebao* 北京師範大學學報 1987.2: 59–62.

Chiang Kai-shek 蔣介石 (Jiang Jieshi). *Zhongguo zhi mingyun* 中國之命運 (China's Destiny). Chongqing: Zhongzheng shuju, 1943.

——. *Jiang Jieshi quanji* 蔣介石全集 (The Collected Works of Chiang Kai-shek). Shanghai: Wenhua bianyi guan, 1937.

——. "Xing de daoli" 行的道理 (The principle of practice). *Lixing Zhexue* 力行哲學, 1940. See *ZLHB* 3, II, 100–106.

——. "Zhexue yu jiaoyu duiyu qingnian de guanxi" 哲學與教育對於青年的關係 (The relationship of philosophy and education to the youth). See *ZLHB* 3, II, 107–113.

Chu Wanzhong 儲皖中. "Lun ren de zhutixing de fazhan yu xiandai jiaoyu zhutixing yuanze de jianli" 論人的主體性的發展與現代教育主體性原則的建立 (On the development of subjectivity and the establishment of the principle of subjectivity in contemporary education). *Beijing shifan daxue xuebao* 北京師範大學學報 1989.4: 75-81.

Cohen, Morris R., and Ernest Nagel. *An Introduction to Logic and Scientific Method.* New York: Harcourt Brace Jovanovich, 1934. Reprinted as "Scientific Method" in Melvin Rader, *The Enduring Questions.* New York: Holt Rinehart and Winston, 1980.

Cong Weixi 叢維熙. "Fenglei yan" 風淚眼 (Eyes with tears), in *Quanguo youxiu zhongpian xiaoshuo pingxuan huojiang zuopinji, 1985–86* 全國優秀中篇小說評選獲獎作品集 (Collection of nationwide prize-winning novellas, 1985–86). Beijing: Zuojia chubanshe, 1988.

Cornford, Francis M. *Plato's Timaeus.* New York: Library of Liberal Arts, 1959.

Crombie, A.C. *Science, Optics, and Music in Medieval and Early Modern Thought.* London: Hambledon Press, 1990.

Deng Xiaoping 鄧小平. "Guanche tiaozheng fangzhen, baozheng anding tuanjie" 貫徹調整方針，保證安定團結 (Guidelines for implementing and regulating, protecting and securing unity). In *Deng Xiaoping wenxuan* 鄧小平文選 (Selected writings of Deng Xiaoping). Beijing: Renmin chubanshe, 1983.

DeWoskin, K. J., and J. I.Crump, trans. *In Search of the Supernatural: The Written Record.* Stanford: Stanford University Press, 1996.

Doyal, Len, and Roger Harris. *Empiricism, Explanation, and Rationality.* London: Routledge and Kegan Paul, 1986.

Feng Weiguo 馮蔚國. "Lixing zhexue yu lunli gaizao" 力行哲學與倫理改造 (The philosophy of practice and the reform of ethics). *Xin renshi* 新認識 1941.11: 15. In *ZLHBJX* 18, 32–36

Feng Youlan 馮友蘭. *Xin lixue* 新理學 (New rationalistic philosophy). *Feng Youlan xueshu jinghua lu* 馮友蘭學術精華錄 (A select record of the scholarly writings of Feng Youlan). Beijing: Beijing shifan xueyuan chubanshe, 1988.

——. *Zhongguo zhexueshi xinbian* 中國哲學史新編 [Selections from] (New edition of the history of Chinese philosophy). In his *Feng Youlan xueshu jinghua lu.* 1988.

——. *Zhongguo zhexueshi xinbian* 中國哲學史新編 (New edition of the history of Chinese philosophy). Vol. 5 (of 7). Beijing: Renmin chubanshe, 1988.

——. *Sansong tang zixu* 三松堂自序 (My intellectual autobiography). Beijing: Sanlian shushe, 1984.

Gould, Stephen Jay. *Hen's Teeth and Horses Toes.* New York: W.W. Norton, 1983.

Gui Yang 貴陽 et al. "Women shehui zhong ren zenma yang bei ' moshihua' le" 我們社會中的人怎樣被"模式化"了 (How people in our society have been 'standardized'). *ZGQN,* 1980.9: 12–14.

Guo Zhan. "The Course of Human Subjectivity." *Social Sciences in China.*1987.4, 207–212.

Han Jingting 韓靜霆. "Shichang jiaoluo de huangdi" 市場角落的皇帝 (The emperor in the corner of the market). *Quanguo youxiu zhongpian xiaoshuo pingxuan huojiang zuopinji, 1983–84* 全國優秀中篇小說評選獲獎作品集 (Collection of nationwide prize-winning novellas, 1983–84). Beijing: Zuojia chubanshe, 1986.

He Lin 賀麟. "Zhi xing wenti di taolun yu fahui" 知行問題的討論與發揮 (A discussion and elaboration of the question of knowledge and action). In He Lin, *Dangdai Zhongguo zhexue* 當代中國哲學 (Contemporary Chinese philosophy) in *ZJSXP,* 70–116.

——. "Dushu yu sixiang" 讀書與思想 (Reading and thinking). In *Wenhua yu rensheng* 文化與人生 (Culture and life). Taibei: Beiping xian chubanshe, 1973, 254–257.

——. "Jindai weixinlun jianshi" 近代唯心論簡釋 (A brief interpretation of modern idealism). In *Zhexue yu zhexueshi lunwenji* 哲學與哲學史論文集 (Collection of works on philosophy and the history of philosophy). 1934. Reprint. Beijing: Sangwu yinshuguan, 1990.

——. "Shikong yu chao shikong"時空與超時空 (Space and time and transcending space and time). *Zhexue pinglun* 哲學評論 4 (1940). See *ZLHB* 3, V, 123–39.

——. Wulun guanian de xin jiantao 五倫觀念的新檢討 (A new investigation of the concept of the five relationships). *Wenhua yu rensheng* 文化與人生 11 (1947). See *ZLHB* 3, V, 76–81.

Hobart, Alice Tisdale. *Oil for the Lamps of China.* New York: Bantam Books, 1945.

Hu Haibo 胡海波. "Shehui zhuti huodong de fangfalun gouxiang" 社會主體活動的方法論構想 (Thinking through the methodology [for research] on the activity of social subjects). *Dongbei shifan daxue xuebao,* 東北師範大學學報 1989.1: 7–12.

Hu Qiaomu 胡橋木. "Guanyu rendao zhuyi he yihua wenti" 關於人道主義和異化問題 (On the question of humanism and alienation). *Hongqi* 紅旗 1984.2: 2–28.

Hu Shi 胡適. "Zhi nan, xing yi bu yi— Sun Zhongshan xiansheng de ' xing yi zhi nan' shuo shuping" 知難行亦不易 — 孫中山先生的'行易知難'說述評 (If knowledge is difficult, action also is not easy — A review of Mr. Sun

Yat-sen's theory that 'action is easy but knowledge is difficult'). *Renquan lunji* 人權論集, 1931: 8. See *ZLHBXJ*, XVI, 205–210.

Hu Yiguan 胡一貫. "Lixing zhexue zhi xin jijie" 力行哲學之新擊節 (A new appreciation of the philosophy of practice). *Wenhua xianfeng* 文化先鋒, 9 (1943). See *ZLHB* 3, II, 133–138.

Huang, Ray. *1587: A Year of No Significance: The Ming Dynasty in Decline*. New Haven: Yale University Press, 1981.

Huang Wenshan 黃文山. *Weishenglun de lishiguan* 唯生論的歷史關 (The historical perspective of vitalism). Taibei: Shangwu yinshuguan, 1982.

Jiang Shan 江山. *Ma'ersasi "Renkou lun" he "Xin renkou lun" de piping* 馬爾薩斯人口論和新人口論的批判 (A critique of Malthus' "Theory of Population" and of "A New Theory of Population"). Shanghai: Shanghai renmin chubanshe, 1958.

Jin Yuelin 金岳霖. *Zhishilun* 知識論 (On Knowledge). Beijing: Shangwu yinshuguan, 1983.

Kwok, Daniel W.Y. *Scientism in Chinese Thought, 1900–1950*. New Haven: Yale University Press, 1965.

Lau, D.C., trans. *Mencius*. Middlesex, England: Penguin, 1970.

——. *Lao Tzu: Tao Te Ching*. Baltimore: Penguin Books, 1963.

Li Deshun. "On the Unity of Truth and Value." *Social Sciences in China* 1985.4: 147–148.

Li Xinsheng 李辛生, and Li Xiaolu 李小魯. "Jiazhi fanchou ying yinru renshilun" 價值范疇應引入認識論 (Introducing the category of value into epistemology). *Huanan shifan daxue xuebao* 南華師範大學學報 1987.1: 1–6.

Li Zehou 李澤厚. *Zhongguo jindai sixiang shi lun* 中國近代思想史論 (Essays on the history of modern Chinese philosophy). Beijing: Xinhua shuju, 1986.

——. "The Philosophy of Kant and a Theory of Subjectivity," in A.T. Tymieniecka, ed., *Analecta Husserliana*. Leiden: Reidel, 1986: 135–149.

——. *Pipan zhexue de pipan* 批判哲學的批判 (A critique of critical philosophy) Beijing: Renmin chubanshe, 1984.

Li Zhilin 李志林. "Lun Zhongguo chuantong siwei fangshi de liangchongxing ji biange de nanjuxing" 論中國傳統思維方式的兩種性及變革的難巨性 (On the twofold character of traditional Chinese thinking and the difficulties in reforming it). *Zhexue yanjiu* 哲學研究, 1989.7: 22–25.

Li Zhisui. *The Private Life of Chairman Mao*. Trans. Tai Hung-chao with editorial assistance of Anne F. Thurston. New York: Random House, 1994.

Liang Shuming 梁漱溟. *Xiangcun jianshe lilun* 鄉村建設理論 (The theory of rural construction). 1934. In *Liang Shuming xueshu jinghua lu* 梁漱溟學術精華綠 (A record of the core scholarly teachings of Liang Shuming). Beijing: Beijing shifan xueyuan chubanshe, 1988.

Lin Fang 林方. *Xinling de kunhuo yu zijiu* 心靈的困惑與自救 (The puzzle and salvation of the psyche). Liaoning: Liaoning renmin chubanshe, 1989.

——. "Comments on Western Humanistic Psychology." *Social Sciences in China* 1985.3: 168–172.

——. "Makesi zhuyi he renben xinlixue" 馬克思主義和人本心理學 (Marxism and humanistic psychology), *Xinlixue xuebao* 心理學學報 1982.2: 1–16.

Lin Jianhan 林堅寒. "Zongcai xing de zhexue tanyuan"總裁行的哲學探源 (An exploration of the Director-General' s philosophy of ' practice'). *Shidai jingshen* 時代精神, 3 (1943). See *ZLHB* 3, II, 200–203.

Liu Baiwen 劉百汶 et al. "Xiandai shehui: chongxin renzheng ziwo" 現代社會: 重新認證自我 (Contemporary society–A renewed authentication of the self). *ZGQN* 1992.9: 12–13.

Liu Zaifu 劉再复. *Lun wenxue de zhutixing* 論文學的主體性 (On subjectivity in literature). Ha'erbin: Heilongjiang jiaoyu chubanshe, 1988, 72 –127.

Longino, Helen E. *Science as Social Knowledge.* Princeton: Princeton University Press, 1990.

Lukes, Steven. *Individualism.* New York: Harper and Row, 1973.

Ma Yinchu 馬寅初. *Xin renkou lun* 新人口論 (A new theory of population). Beijing: Beijing chubanshe, 1979.

——. "Woguo renkou wenti yu fazhan shengchanli de guanxi" 我國人口問題與發展生產力的關係 (The relation between our country' s population and the development of productive capacity). *Dagongbao* 大公報, May 9, 1957.

Mann, Susan. *Local Merchants and the Chinese Bureaucracy, 1750–1950.* Stanford: Stanford University Press, 1987.

Mao Zedong 毛澤東. "Yanjiu lunxianqu" 研究淪陷區 (An investigation of enemy-held territory). 1939. In *ZXZJC*.II, 993–995.

——. "Some Questions Concerning Methods of Leadership." 1943. In *Selected Works of Mao Zedong*. Beijing: Foreign Languages Press, 1965.

——. "' Qida' gongzuo fangzhen" ' 七大' 工作方針 (Work guidelines for the Seventh All-Peoples Congress). 1945. In *ZXZJC*.II, 1010–1021.

——. "Ziyou shi biran de renshi he shijie de gaizao" 自由是必然的認識和世界的改造 (Freedom is knowledge of necessity and changing the world). 1941. In *ZXZJC*.II, 997–998.

——. "Guanyu nongcun diaocha" 關於農村調查 (On the investigation of rural villages), 1941. In *ZXZJC*.II, 1000–1005.

Meisner, Maurice. *Mao's China and After.* New York: The Free Press, 1986.

Metzger, Thomas A. "The Organizational Capabilities of the Ch'ing State in the Field of Commerce: The Liang-huai Salt Monopoly, 1740–1840." In *Economic Organization in Chinese Society.* William E. Willmott, ed. Stanford: Stanford University Press, 1972.

Misra, Kalpana. "Rethinking Marxism in Post-Mao China: The Erosion of Official Ideology, 1978–84." Ph.D. dissertation, University of Michigan, 1992.

Munro, Donald J. "One-Minded Hierarchy versus Interest Group Pluralism: Two Chinese approaches to Conflict." In *New Approaches to Conflict in World Politics.* William Zimmerman and Harold Jacobson, eds. Ann Arbor: University of Michigan Press, 1994.

——. *Images of Human Nature: A Sung Portrait.* Princeton: Princeton University Press, 1988.

——. *Individualism and Holism: Studies in Conducian and Taoistic Values.* Ann Arbor: Center for Chinese Studies, The University of Michigan, 1985.

——. "The Chinese View of Alienation." *China Quarterly* 59 (July-September 1974): 580–82.

——. *The Concept of Man in Contemporary China* (Ann Arbor: University of Michigan Press, 1977).

Ng Chin-keong. *Trade and Society: The Amoy Network on the China Coast, 1683–1735*. Singapore: Singapore University Press, 1983.

Pan Shu 潘菽. Xinlixue jianzha 心理學簡札 (Brief notes on psychology). Beijing: Renmen chubanshe, 1984.

——. "Jiajin gaizao xinlixue wei quanmian kaichuang shehuizhuyi xiandaihua jianshe de xinjumian fuwu." 加緊改造心理學爲全面開創社會主義現代化的新局面服務 (Speed up the reconstruction of psychology to serve the new situation in the construction of socialist modernization). *Xinli kexue tongxun* 心理科學通訊 (Information on psychological sciences) 1983.2, 5–9.

Plamenatz, John. *Man and Society*. 2 vols. New York: McGraw-Hill, 1969.

Qin Xiaoyi 秦孝儀, ed. *Zhanshi jiaoyu fangzhen* 戰時教育方針 (Guiding principles for wartime education). Taibei: Zhongyang wenwu gongyingshe, 1976.

Reardon-Anderson, James. *The Study of Change: Chemistry in China, 1840–1949.* Cambridge: Cambridge University Press, 1991.

Rowe, William T. *Hankow: Commerce and Society in a Chinese City, 1796–1889.* Stanford: Stanford University Press, 1984.

Schram, Stuart R. "Mao Tse-tung and the Theory of Permanent Revolution," 1958–69. *China Quarterly* 46 (April-June 1971): 221–224.

——, ed. *The Scope of State Power in China.* London: School of Oriental and African Studies, 1985.

Schurman, Franz. *Ideology and Organization in China.* Berkeley: University of California Press, 1966.

"Shenke de jiaoxun" 深刻的教訓 (A profound lesson). *Xinhua yuekan* 新華月刊 1980.8: 69.

Shiba Yoshinobu. *Commerce and Society in Sung China.* Mark Elvin, trans. Ann Arbor: University of Michigan, Center for Chinese Studies, 1970.

"Song Zhenming jiu ' Bohai erhao' zhuanjingchuan fanchen shigu de jiantao" 宋振明就'渤海二號'井船翻沈事故的檢討 (Song Zhenming' s self-criticism concerning the Bohai No. 2 platform). *Xinhua yuekan* 新華月刊 1980.8: 70–73.

Song Renqiong 宋任窮. "Yong xin dangzhang jiaoyu dangyuan, wei zhengdang zuohao sixiang zhunbei" 用新黨章教育黨員爲整黨做好思想準備 (Use new Party rules to educate Party members, do a good job of thought preparation for the entire Party). *Hongqi* 紅旗 1982.24: 16–20.

Sun Yat-sen 孫中山. *Sun Zhongshan quanshu* 孫中山全書 (Complete works of Sun Yat-sen). Guangzhou: Guangyi shuju, 1936.

——. *Sun Wen xueshuo.* 孫文學說 (Writings of Sun Yat-sen) Taipei: Zhongyang wenwu gongyingshe, 1957.

Tian Hanzu 田漢族. "Lun xuesheng zhutixing zuoyong fahui de jiben yuanze" 論學生主體作用發揮的基本原則 (On the basic principle of the function of giving play to the student' s subjectivity). *Jiaoyu yanjiu* 教育研究 1991.8: 116–120.

Wakeman, Frederic, Jr. "The Civil Society and Public Sphere Debate," *Modern China* 19.2 (April, 1993): 108–137.

Wang Daojun 王道俊, and Guo Wen' an 郭文安. "Shilun jiaoyu de zhutixing" 試論教育的主體性 (A tentative discussion on subjectivity in education). *Huadong shifan daxue xuebao* 華東師範大學學報 1990.4: 33–40.

Wang Kunqing 王坤慶. "Lun jiaoyu jiazhi zhong ren de jiazhi diwei" 論教育價值中人的價值地位 (On the position of human values within educational values). *Huadong shifan daxue xuebao* 華東師範大學學報 1991.2: 49–56.

Wang Meng 王蒙. "Dongtian de huati" 冬天的話題 (A winter' s tale). *Xiaoshuojia* 小說家, 1985.2: 203-226.

Wang Pengling 王鵬令. "Mianxiang zhuti he kexue" 面向主體和科學 (Toward the subject and science). *Zhongguo shehui kexue* 中國社會科學 1987.3: 68–72.

——. "Toward the Subject and Science: Two Tendencies in the Study of Dialectical Materialism in China over the Past Decade." *Social Sciences in China* 1988.2: 9–16.

Wang Ruoshui. "On the Marxist Philosophy or Man." *FBIS*, Chi. 86–114 of July 23 and 142 of July 24, 1986.

Watson, Burton, trans. *Hsun Tzu: Basic Writings*. New York: Columbia University Press, 1963.

Will, Pierre-Etienne. "State Intervention in the Administration of a Hydraulic Infrastructure: The Example of Hubei Province in Late Imperial Times." In *The Scope of State Power in China*. Stuart R. Schram, ed. London: School of Oriental and African Studies, 1985.

Xiong Shili 熊十力. *Xin weishilun* 新唯識論 (New idealism). Beijing: Zhonghua shuju, 1985.

——. *Xin weishilun* 新唯識論 (New idealism). Taibei: Guangwen shuju, 1962.

——. *Zhongguo lishi jianghua* 中國歷史講話 (Lectures on the history of China). 1939. Reprint. Taibei: Ming wen shuju, 1984.

Yang Jianye 楊建業. *Ma Yinchu zhuan* 馬寅初傳 (Biography of Ma Yinchu). Beijing: Zhongguo qingnian chubanshe, 1986.

Yang Shi. "The Historical Status of the Traditional Chinese Theory of Man." *Social Sciences in China* 1989.4: 55.

Yap Key-chong. "Western Wisdom in the Mind' s Eye of a Westernized Chinese Lay Buddhist: The Thought of Chang Tung-sun, 1886–1962." Ph.D dissertation, University of Oxford, 1989.

Yuan Guiren 袁貴仁. "Jiazhi yu renshi" 價值與認識 (Values and cognition). In *Beijing shifan daxue xuebao* 北京師範大學學報 1985.3: 47–57.

Zhang Shiying 張世英. "Xifang zhexueshizhong zhutixing yuanze de fazhan yu Zhongguo zhexueshizhong guanyu ren de lilun" 西方哲學史中主體性原則的發展與中國哲學史中關於人的理論 (The development of the principle of subjectivity in the history of Western philosophy, and the theory of man in the history of Chinese philosophy). In *Ren yu ziran* 人與自然 (Man and nature). Philosophy Department of Peking Univer-sity, ed. Beijing: Beijing daxue chubanshe, 1987.

Zhang Xuezhi 張學智. "Lun He Lin dui Sibinnuosha (Spinoza) sixiang de xishou yu gaizao" 論賀麟對斯賓諾莎思想的吸收與改造 (He Lin' s absorption from and reformulation of Spinoza' s thought). *Wen shi zhe* 文史哲 (Shandong) 1990.1: 34–39.

——. "Lun He Lin de ' Xi zhe Dong zhe, xin tong li tong.' " 論賀麟的 '西哲東哲, 心同理同' (On He Lin' s ' Merging of Western and Chinese philosophy and equation of mind and principle'), unpublished paper.

Zheng Guoping 鄭國平. "Jiazhi zai renshizhong de zuoyong" 價值在認識中的作用 (The function of values in knowing). In *Zhexue yanjiu* 哲學研究 1986.7: 28–29.

Zhongbao yuekan 中報月刊 (Zhongbao monthly) 75 Hong Kong, 1986.

Zhongguo guomindang zhongyang weiyuanhui 中國國民黨中央委員會. *San min zhuyi* 三民主義 (The Three People' s Principles). Taibei: Zhongyang wenwu gongyingshe, 1985.

Zhongguo xiandai zhexue shi jiaoxue cailiao xuanji 中國現代哲學史教學資料選輯 (Selected academic source materials for the study of the history of modern Chinese philosophy). Beijing: Beijing daxue chubanshe, 1988.

Zhongguo xiandai zhexue shi ziliao huibian 中國現代哲學史資料匯編 (Compilation of source materials in the history of modern Chinese philosophy), Liaoning: Philosophy Section of Liaoning University, 1981.

Zhongguo xiandai zhexue shi ziliao huibian xuji 中國現代哲學史資料匯編續集 (Continuation of the compilation of source materials in the history of modern Chinese philosophy). Liaoning: Philosophy Section of Liaoning University, 1984.

Zhou Guoping 周國平. "Ren de huodong he wanzheng de renxing"人的活動和完整的人性 (Human activity and the integrative nature of man). In *Rendao zhuyi wenti wenji* 人道主義問題文集 (A collection of problems in humanism). Liaoning: Liaoning renmin chubanshe, 1985, 107–133.

Zhou Haobo 周浩波. "Shilun jiaoyu guocheng zhong de ertong zhutixing" 試論教育過程中的兒童主體性 (A tentative discussion on childhood subjectivity within the educational process). *Jiaoyu yanjiu* 教育研究 1989.6: 16–19.

Zhu Xi 朱熹. *Huian xiansheng Zhu Wengong wenji* 晦菴先生朱文公集 (Collection of literary works of Master Zhu). In *Sibu congkan* 四部叢刊, XXXIII.

Zichan jieji xueshu sixiang pipan cankao ziliao 資產階級學術思想批判參考資料 (Source materials for the critique of capitalist academic thought). Beijing: Shangwu yinshuguan, 1959.

Zimmerman, William, and Harold Jacobson, eds. *New Approaches to Conflict in World Politics.* Ann Arbor: University of Michigan Press, 1994.

Index

Printed and bound by CPI Group (UK) Ltd, Croydon, CR0 4YY
13/04/2025
14656507-0005